Praise for WRITING RADAR

★ "An excellent guide . . . And while the book is directed at serious writers in the making, there's enough exaggeration and grossness to keep readers laughing."
—*Publishers Weekly*, **starred review**

★ "Never less than entertaining and sometimes laugh-out-loud funny, [this is] a focused, fun, and uncommonly useful guide." —*Booklist*, **starred review**

★ "A must for aspiring writers."
—*School Library Journal*, **starred review**

★ "Gantos's journey as a young writer learning his craft and the stories he actually wrote in middle school, all told with his characteristic humor, will appeal to fans of his novels whether or not they aspire to a writing career. Teachers will also find Gantos's breakdown on the creation of a story valuable for teaching critical reading as well as writing skills." —*VOYA*, **starred review**

"A standout among writing guides, valuable for its sage and friendly encouragement and for the sheer fun of hanging out with Jack." —*Kirkus Reviews*

"With humor and swift pacing, the author of the Joey Pigza books and *Dead End in Norvelt* spills all of his writing secrets about making stories out of everyday life . . . [*Writing Radar*] will probably make you want to read Gantos's stories as well as to create your own." —*The Washington Post*

Writing Radar

By **Jack Gantos**

Heads or Tails: Stories from the Sixth Grade

Jack's New Power: Stories from a Caribbean Year

Desire Lines

Jack's Black Book

Joey Pigza Swallowed the Key

Jack on the Tracks: Four Seasons of Fifth Grade

Joey Pigza Loses Control

Hole in My Life

What Would Joey Do?

Jack Adrift: Fourth Grade Without a Clue

The Love Curse of the Rumbaughs

I Am Not Joey Pigza

Dead End in Norvelt

From Norvelt to Nowhere

The Key That Swallowed Joey Pigza

The Trouble in Me

*Writing Radar: Using Your Journal to Snoop Out
and Craft Great Stories*

WRITING RADAR

TRUST ME!

TRUST YOURSELF!

Using Your Journal to Snoop Out and Craft Great Stories

Jack Gantos

Think Ink

SQUARE
FISH

Farrar Straus Giroux

New York

SQUARE
FISH

An imprint of Macmillan Publishing Group, LLC
175 Fifth Avenue, New York, NY 10010
mackids.com

Our books may be purchased in bulk for promotional, educational, or business
use. Please contact your local bookseller or the Macmillan Corporate and
Premium Sales Department at (800) 221-7945 ext. 5442 or by email at
MacmillanSpecialMarkets@macmillan.com.

Library of Congress Cataloging-in-Publication Data

Names: Gantos, Jack, author.
Title: Writing radar : using your journal to snoop out and craft great stories /
    Jack Gantos.
Description: New York : Farrar Straus Giroux, 2017. | Description based on
    print version record and CIP data provided by publisher; resource not viewed.
Identifiers: LCCN 2016057821 (print) | LCCN 2017018550 (ebook) | ISBN
    978-1-250-22298-5 (paperback) | ISBN 978-0-374-30457-7 (ebook)
Subjects: LCSH: Authorship—Vocational guidance—Juvenile literature. |
    Creative writing—Vocational guidance—Juvenile literature.
Classification: LCC PN159 (ebook) | LCC PN159 .G36 2017 (print) |
    DDC 808.02—dc23
LC record available at https://lccn.loc.gov/2016057821

Originally published in the United States by Farrar Straus Giroux
First Square Fish edition, 2019
Book designed by Andrew Arnold
Square Fish logo designed by Filomena Tuosto

1   3   5   7   9   10   8   6   4   2

AR: 6.1 / LEXILE: 940L

For Anne and Mabel
and Nacho & Scootch

Contents

Before Writing, There Was Storytelling xi

1   Trust Me 3

2   Getting Started 8

3   The Best Journal in the World Is Yours 13

4   Turning On and Fine-Tuning Your Writing

     Radar 25

5   Story Hunting and Gathering 29

6   The Writing Journal in Action 43

7   "I'll Kill You," Said My Sister 48

8   The Oath 61

9   Blank Slate 65

10   Story Maps 73

11   Action *and* Emotion 84

12   Power! 94

13   Good Habits Lead to Great Inspiration 101

14   Story Structure and Story Elements 110

15 Putting My Oath to the Test 117

16 The Follower. 125

17 Breaking It Down. 142

18 My First Reader Teaches Me a Lesson 153

19 Focused Drafts 164

20 A Parting Surprise 173

A Final Word 193

Writing Connections 195

Before Writing, There Was Storytelling

VISITOR PASS
DATE: OCTOBER 28TH
NAME: Jack Gantos

So, let me tell you a story about how stories happen to me all day long and why keeping a journal has been my greatest writing tool ever since I was a kid.

The other day I spoke to students at a school in Boston about how to set up their writing journals. Everything about the school was bright and shiny with furniture polish and fresh paint. Each room was well organized, and so neat and tidy the kids looked like mannequins as they sat motionless with their hands clasped together and wide eyes zeroed in on mine. They didn't twitch or wiggle. They didn't wince when I told them stories about the fountains of blood squirting out of me like lawn sprinklers after I pulled warts off my body with rusty pliers. They didn't blink when I told them about how I was shot across my neighbors' yard on their homemade human catapult. Nothing got a rise out of these kids, but I was determined to inspire them to show some *emotion*—some *pleasure*—some storytelling joy! I told them about riding bikes off the neighbors' roof and into their swimming pool, sticking forks into electric sockets and shattering my fingernails, roller-skating through flaming hula hoops, eating cockroaches—nothing worked. These kids were not human. I glanced at their teacher for a clue as to what had turned these kids into sculpted zombies. She avoided my eyes and stood in a corner with slumped shoulders as if she were a defeated flag on a pole.

This utter lack of emotion was something I had seen before. But where? When? I felt as if I had written about it in another life, as if I was living an event all over again.

This feeling of déjà vu had started earlier, when I had entered the school's front office and signed in as a guest speaker. The secretary had given me a sticky VISITOR pass to slap onto my jacket lapel. From experience, I knew not to put it onto my jacket because sometimes the glue didn't come off properly and left behind a permanent ugly smudge. I held the sticky pass by the corner and planned to slap it onto the bottom of some kid's desk when I got the chance.

At that moment, a strong bleachy smell began to blow from the overhead air vent. I took one sniff and my eyes began to water. I spotted a box of tissues on the office counter. As I reached forward, the secretary saw my hand.

"Not so fast," she advised. "You'd better read the tissue box pledge."

On the side of the box was taped a three-by-five card that said:

> *I don't want an* issue
> *So before you take a* tissue
> *More than one is an* excess
> *Blow your nose without a* mess
> —Poetic advice from: MISS FIDELITY

I carefully took just one tissue. As I dabbed at my nose I raised my eyes and noticed a radiant gold-framed portrait of the tanned principal, *MISS FIDELITY*, staring down into my eyes.

She was in a yellow suit, and across her neck hung a triple strand of glowing pearls that harmonized with the luminous sheen of her pearly smile. Her pewter hair was piled upward on her head and sculpted into the shape of an old school bell. Between her red well-scrubbed hands she held a book titled *There Is Always a Better Way*.

I wonder who wrote that book, I said to myself. My guess was soon confirmed.

I was buzzed through the office security door and entered the main hallway, where the sunny Miss Fidelity waited to welcome me with her hand extended.

I marched forward, and as I did so my sticky name tag broke away and floated toward the floor. It landed glue-side down, and in my haste to be polite I stepped on it as I shook her hand.

"Thank you for inviting me into your school," I said warmly.

"I hate to begin a friendship by asking for a favor," she said directly, "but could you pick up your fallen name tag?"

"Sure," I replied, and dutifully squatted down. But the name tag had flatly adhered to the floor. I tried to dig a fingernail under one corner and peel it up, but I only succeeded in tearing away thin shreds of paper.

"Can't get a grip on it?" she remarked impatiently. "Well, there is always a better way."

"I'm sure there is," I replied, and smiled awkwardly as I hopped up.

"Now, if you will excuse me," she said, "I have to supervise the morning announcements. Today our student Respect Team is performing." Then she gave a final harsh glance toward the stuck name tag before marching into the office.

A moment later, "Good morning, students!" boomed from the ceiling speakers and out the open doors of the classrooms. Her no-nonsense voice was as severe as barbed wire. "Let us all start our day by shouting the school's Respect Pledge along with our Respect Cheer Team!"

Once again, I felt as if I was living my past all over again. But I had no time to reflect on it because the Respect Team took the microphone and shouted, "*R* is for respect!"

"Respect" echoed down the shiny hallway.

"*E* is for effort" was next.

That was followed by a rousing "*S* is for studying!"

"And *P* is for perseverance!"

"*E* is for energy!"

"*C* is for caring!" (I thought I heard some kid shout out "cleaning!")

"*T* is for teamwork!"

When they had finished, Miss Fidelity took the microphone. "Could someone send a Respect Ambassador to the main hallway with a sharp-edged scraper?" she said. "We have an *issue* on the floor."

When she said "Respect Ambassador" I suddenly realized why I felt I had lived this day once already—because, in a way, I had.

• • •

That day I spoke to several groups of students at Miss Fidelity's school, and when I finished I eagerly dashed home and began to search through my collection of old journals. It didn't take long to find what I was looking for.

I was in fifth grade when I wrote about being a school "Respect Detective." I was the new kid at school that year and on my first day the principal called me into her office. "I have a job for you," she said. "Nobody knows you yet and you don't know the other kids, so you will be the perfect detective for me."

"Detective" didn't sound very friendly to me. But I was a pretty good snoop. If you keep a diary, you must be a bit of a snoop in order to sneak up on people, listen to what they say, watch what they do, and write it all down.

The principal continued. "There are two things going on in this school that I'm determined to stop," she said with her voice full of determination. "First, some kid is chewing gum and sticking it under the desks and cafeteria tables and sinks in the bathroom—everywhere. I scraped off a dozen samples of gum and showed them to my dentist. He said the tooth pattern in the gum belongs to one kid—and I want you to catch that kid."

"Okay," I said as she handed me a sample of chewed

gum so I could match it to the dental profile of the culprit.

"And the other problem I have is this," she said, and pointed toward her window. "Across the playing field is a fence and on the other side of the fence is a pet cemetery, and someone has been stealing flowers off the animal graves and leaving them in front of the cute teacher's locker in the teachers' lounge. Maybe it's the same person, but you have to catch who is doing it!"

"Yes, ma'am," I replied, and went to work to find the culprits.

Until I was in that "zombie" school in Boston, I had forgotten about my fifth-grade school and how the principals were exactly alike. They banned fun and had so many rules and regulations, they turned the kids into zombies. But now that I was back home with my old journal, that school year became crystal clear as I read about all the snooping I had done. My fifth-grade writing was a mess, but the wild ideas were terrific. Back then, I just didn't know how to turn great ideas and all the zombie details into complete stories, and the Respect Detective writing remained lost inside the journal. Now I knew how to take it out of my journal, polish it up, and turn it into a *winner*.

In fifth grade I stayed after school scraping all the

ancient gum off the undersides of the desks until I found one desk with about a hundred hunks of fresh gum stuck under it—and the tooth pattern in the gum matched the sample the principal had given me. The next day I went up to the kid and explained to him why he had to quit before the principal killed him. Later, he became my best friend. He was the only kid who wasn't a zombie.

After I solved that problem I found the pet cemetery flower thief right away. I got up extra early one morning and in the dark walked to the cemetery and hid behind a large stone goat. The sun was rising when I saw a man jump the schoolyard fence and grab some fresh flowers from a cat's gravestone. Just as quickly he jumped back over the fence and ran across the schoolyard and through the janitor's back door, which led to the teachers' lounge and lockers. I recognized him right away— it was the gym teacher!

That day I slipped a note into his locker: "I know you are the flower thief! Stop it or else! Sincerely, The Respect Detective."

We never had another gum or flower issue again. And my job as the Respect Detective was over! Thank goodness.

As an adult writer, my student journals still inspire me. Some days I slowly flip through the pages and I never fail to find something to write about—something small or large or slightly crazy or heartfelt, some event or feeling that I would have forgotten forever if I had not written it down. I'm so glad I did. Without my journals, I would not have fifty published books with my name on them—books that I am proud to have written.

Good luck with your journals—they are the beginning of your career as a writer. And now, turn the page and I will give you the best advice ever on how to start snooping out and writing your own great stories.

Writing Radar

1

Trust
Me

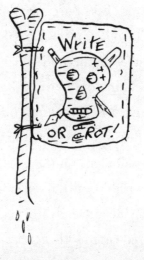

I'm a writer and I'm on your side.

There comes a time when every good reader decides they want to write a book, so I'm writing this book just for you. You have chosen to read this book because you want to be a brilliant writer, and I chose to write this book because I want you to be the *best* brilliant writer. I want you to take advantage of your every writerly thought, every clever observation, and every powerful emotion to create unforgettable stories that come from the very center of your life and that will live forever in a reader's mind. And you can do it.

Even if you don't think of yourself as a great reader, you know how to read yourself. The words you use to describe the world around you and the world within you are a form of reading. Take the expression "I can read you like a book." Well, you *are* a book on the inside. Writing just turns you inside out, and all your thoughts become words on a page. Think of the word *reading* this way and do not doubt yourself. Everyone has talent, and my aim in this book is to help you develop yours.

In this book I will focus on the greatest tool in every writer's life: the writer's journal—a book that puts you *first* in your writing life and activates your Writing Radar to help you spot and capture the stories you want to tell.

The journal is a basic tool that all writers use. A slender notebook is easy to carry around in your pocket. Plus, it is a tool you can use *very quietly*, which is why it is so effective for when you are sneaking and snooping around the world you live in and capturing uniquely clever story ideas.

I started keeping a journal in fifth grade, and once I got it properly set up and put myself at the center of my writing life, I discovered that stories were taking shape around me all day long. My job in this book is to show you how to set up your own journal to capture, organize, and polish the great stories that are taking shape around *you* all day long.

Once you get your journal going and see how brilliant you are, then you'll want to keep it going. There is no greater motivation than the taste of self-made success.

Just so you know I'm not some big talker about writing books, let me give you a little background about me. After keeping journals and dreaming about becoming a professional writer all through school, I went to college for creative writing. While there, I published my first book, *Rotten Ralph*, in 1976. It is a picture book illustrated by my friend Nicole Rubel and based on a menacing pet we shared. *Rotten Ralph* is still in print, and I have published more than fifty books since then. A good number are picture books, but I also have five volumes of short stories that I took from my early kid journals about a boy named Jack Henry. (I changed the name of the character in the stories from Jack Gantos to Jack Henry to keep from embarrassing my mother—well, to keep from embarrassing my entire family.) I've also written five novels about a funny, bighearted, but wired kid named Joey Pigza; a couple of wild autobiographical novels set in my hometown of Norvelt in western Pennsylvania; and two books about some trouble I got into during and after high school.

In short, I have written everything from picture books, to upper-elementary and middle school novels and collections of short stories, to high school books—and they all began in my journals.

Aside from publishing my own books, I was a college creative writing professor for twenty years, during which I directed a children's book writing and publishing program that launched the careers of other writers. Plus, I have also visited over a thousand schools, where I have worked directly with tens of thousands of young writers like you on setting up their journals and creative writing projects.

Everything I know about writing stories is in this book. I want to be the best creative writing teacher you ever had, and I'll show you how your basic pen and journal (which may be collecting dust on your desk) will become the essential everyday tools you carry in your pocket in order to capture your true writing voice—a strong voice that will enable you to define both the vastly detailed world that surrounds you and the richly unique world within you.

In this book I will tell you a lot of stories that are full of truths, mayhem, emotion, and personal insights into myself and others. Along the way I'll share my best how-to writing tips so you can see how a story is built, step by step, and then polished to perfection.

I promise you that all of my teaching skills, enthusiasm, and support are just FOR you! TRUST YOURSELF!

Trust me, I want you to succeed, but more important, I want you to TRUST Yourself!

2

Getting Started

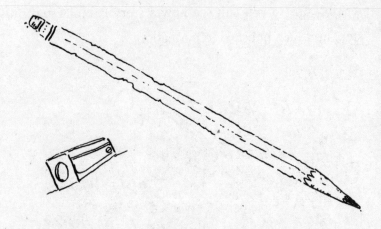

Without lifting a pencil (or chewing on one),
you began your journey to become a writer a long time
ago. It actually began before you could read, when you
were sitting in someone's lap. They read you a storybook—and you liked it! The words and pictures captured
your imagination, and you wanted more. You reached
out and held the book. Then you hugged the book. You
may even have chewed on the book, but certainly you
wanted it read to you over and over so you could memorize

every word and feel the story living inside you like a virus—a friendly book virus.

Well, most of the world's greatest writers started the same way. Someone read them a storybook when they were young, and they, too, were captured by it and wanted more. Then, when they learned to read, they became nonstop readers, and I suspect you are a nonstop reader, too. It's probably impossible for you to count up how many books you have read since you were very young, but I bet you can still remember some of the classics that got you started: *Brown Bear, Brown Bear, What Do You See?* . . . *The Very Hungry Caterpillar* . . . *Harold and the Purple Crayon* . . . *The Snowy Day* . . . *Where the Wild Things Are* . . . *Miss Nelson Is Missing!* . . . *Sylvester and the Magic Pebble* . . . *The Stinky Cheese Man and Other Fairly Stupid Tales* . . . *Frog and Toad Are Friends* . . . *Arnie the Doughnut* . . .

And then as you got older, along came *James and the Giant Peach* . . . *The Borrowers* . . . *The Cricket in Times Square* . . . *Half-Magic* . . . *Charlotte's Web* . . . *Island of the Blue Dolphins* . . . *From the Mixed-up Files of Mrs. Basil E. Frankweiler* . . . *Harry Potter and the Sorcerer's Stone* . . . *One Crazy Summer* . . . *Stella by Starlight* . . . *Hatchet* . . . *Under the Blood-Red Sun* . . . *Baseball in April* . . . *Tuck Everlasting* . . . *The Goats* . . . *The Chocolate War* . . . *The Outsiders* . . . *The Wednesday Wars* . . . *Brown Girl*

Dreaming . . . Esperanza Rising . . . Pax . . . Booked . . . (maybe even *Joey Pigza Swallowed the Key*).

Imagine if all of these great books you read and loved, and who knows how many hundreds more, could be stacked up on your bedside table to form an incredibly tall pillar of books. At this very moment, while this book is in your hands, I want you to picture standing on top of that imaginary pillar. Your intense eyes are as bright and observant as lighthouse beacons as you scan your world.

From your towering perch of favorite books, you can

spot brilliant stories popping up and coming to life all around you. Also, from the top of your tall stack of books, you have the ability to shine a light deep into yourself to search out hidden ideas that are just waiting to be discovered and turned into stories.

Reading good books turns on the powerful Writing Radar story-finding talent within you. *Reading* sharpens your eye for discovering keen details and unforgettable images. *Reading* coaches your brain to keep working until you discover the perfect words to describe powerful actions and precise emotions. *Reading* gives you an ear for clever dialogue that makes characters jump off the page and light up the imaginary theater within the reader's mind.

The Power of Reading

When I read a book it reads me in return.
When I finish the last page the book
remains the same, but I am changed
forever.

Even though your world may seem large and mysterious, do not panic. Because when you sit down with a writing journal in your hands the whole untamed world of your raw ideas and imagination will then curl up snugly onto your lap, like a favorite pet.

All writers know that reading quickens your writing talent for describing characters and their actions and their range of emotions. Plus, reading well-organized stories that have a solid beginning, middle, and end helps you structure your stories. But unless you have content—*story material*—and capture a lively story on paper, all your solid creative writing and organizing skills will go to waste and rot.

READING GIVES ME MUSCLES FOR WRITING!

So let's turn to the next chapter and begin to exercise our Writing Radar by finding good story material.

3

The Best Journal in the World Is Yours

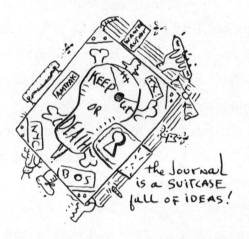

the Journal is a SUITCASE full of IDEAS!

When I open my journal, pick up my pen, and begin to write, I know deep inside me that the journal is the one place I can go to express any thought, be anyone, wear any hat, say any silly thing, say any rowdy thing, and be as loud or as crazy or as wacky as I want to be. It is also where I can be creative and thoughtful, and where I can quietly capture my own raw emotions with just the perfect words.

My journal is a book full of surprises, and if I'm lucky

the writing leads me to discover something new about myself that I can use in a story. In *your* journal I want you to have the same untamed freedom of expression that leads to self-discovery and the thrill of creating "something out of nothing" with your written words.

Today I have more than two hundred journals packed away in boxes. I try every day to do a little purposeful writing in my journal, such as bits of story ideas, imagined conversations, or character notes. But a lot of times I just walk around with a packet of Post-it notes that I scribble on and later stick in my journal. Believe me, not every one of my journal entries is a great, thoughtful, heartfelt, genius moment. Sometimes what I add to my journal is just as mundane as a grocery list for a dinner recipe I'm thinking of, or the title of a book I want to read, or song lyrics that are stuck in my mind, or a thought I have on how to write books. It could be a drawing of my cats. Or even a taped-in picture from something interesting I cut out of a magazine or the morning newspaper.

Working in a journal makes you pay attention to the whole world around you. It makes you aware of good days, bad days, embarrassing days, days when you were dealing with homework, sports, music, friends, enemies, romantic feelings, angry feelings, and so much more.

The journal is the place where you start making connections between how you are growing up, what you know about yourself and others, and how you fit in. It gets you thinking about the connections between *everything*—and it's this sequence of connections between what you see, feel, think, and imagine that builds a story from the beginning, to the middle, to the end. There is no greater tool than the journal for connecting all the dots in your life, so keep your journal-writing tools with you at all times. Trust me, I do.

WRITING TIP.

The more you stuff your journal with the odds and ends of life, the more you find that the odds and ends connect to create complete stories. Try to add to your writing journal every day. I make it a rule to see or hear something interesting, find something interesting, or imagine something interesting that I can either write about or glue into my journal.

Journals are easy to come by. Maybe your parents or grandparents or a teacher gave you one and you are wondering what to do with it (besides hiding it under your bed).

Or maybe you are a kid who has a dozen journals sitting on a shelf and just one unfinished sentence written in each one. I can imagine how tortured you might be when you slip up at home and say to your parents, "I'm bored!"

In a snap they both sing out, "Why don't you go to your room and open your birthday journal and do some writing?"

Argh! Doesn't that crush you? Doesn't that make you want to crawl inside one of your journals and pull the cover down over yourself as if you were settling into your own coffin?

Or what about this: How do you feel when your super-excited teacher rings a little bell on her desk and says with blissful delight, "Class, take out your *fabulous* journals and let's have fifteen minutes of quiet freewriting time"? I bet that sends you into a fifteen-minute cold panic of *What should I write about?* And fifteen minutes later you scramble to write one word: *Help!*

So let's start with the first, most thorny worry that faces most young writers (and older ones, too):

"Nothing interesting ever happens to ME!"

This is the all-ages writer's lament.

Yet, with a little prodding, some well-directed questions, and some prompts, most writers soon find that interesting things do happen to them—and either they were not paying attention or they just didn't fully trust that their personal experiences were worth writing about.

For example, a young girl came up to me after one of

my school presentations and said she wasn't sure if she had anything interesting to write about.

I asked her if she had had a recent embarrassing moment.

"Yes," she replied, and blushed.

And then, with a good bit of hand-wringing, she told me what had happened to her a few months earlier. It was the week when school pictures were taken and she had been preparing to look her best. All her previous ones had been pretty lousy—missing teeth, huge fake smile, blinding shiny spot on forehead, frilly outfit with super-large lace collar—and so this time she was determined to be poised, dignified, and well groomed. She'd just gotten her braces removed and was ready to show off her new smile.

On the big day she chose her most sophisticated outfit and had her thick hair tucked behind her ears so it wouldn't cast a shadow across her face. Still, when her class was called down to the library for the picture session she felt some butterflies in her stomach. She had her big orange comb in hand and as she nervously waited in line she compulsively combed her hair into place. And then disaster struck. Somehow in her combing frenzy the comb got knotted up in her bangs and she couldn't get it unfastened, and suddenly it was her turn to take a seat. Before she knew it, she'd had her picture snapped with the big orange comb hanging down over her forehead and covering her nose.

I listened patiently.

"So," she concluded, "is that worth writing about?" And then she opened her purse and pulled out the picture.

It was a classic.

"Are you kidding?" I declared. "Your story is certainly worth writing about." Then I asked, "Do you have a journal?"

"Yes," she said.

"Then paste the picture in your journal and use it as inspiration to write the story 'The Worst Picture Day Ever.'"

She bit down on her lip. "Thanks," she said. "I just wasn't sure it would be interesting."

I walked away thinking, *If she doesn't use that story, I will.*

I didn't get far down the hall before I was cornered by another student.

"I think I might have something interesting to write about," he said, and stuck his tongue out at me. There was a crusty purple circle right in the middle of it.

"Tell me about how you got that hideous spot," I insisted.

He told me that he'd heard that if you pressed your tongue onto something very, very cold the tongue would stick to it. So one freezing winter day when his parents were away, he went outside to where his hockey goal was set up. He pressed his tongue onto the metal goalpost and proved to himself that he was right—tongues do stick to

cold things! Only now he couldn't remove his tongue and was trapped outside.

A couple hours later his parents came home and saw their son stuck to a metal pole by his tongue. They ran outside and poured warm water on his tongue until he could peel it off. But it left a circular purple crust on his taste buds. His father called it the "birthmark of a misunderstood genius."

Writing Tip:

Never forget: Every painful moment in life is a story waiting to be told.

And on it went. Students lined up to tell me their stories that they were unsure about. But it turned out that these were the most amazing stories of them all. By the end of the day I had heard enough stories to fill a book. But they were not my stories. They belonged to those new young writers who were already scribbling away in their journals and capturing their "most embarrassing moment ever!" or some other powerful or quirky incident that with some writerly thought could be crafted into a great story.

Remember, good stuff to write about is happening to you all the time. So don't panic. When your Writing Radar spots a hot story and goes off like a fire alarm, just pull out your journal and a pen and write it down.

I do the same thing. Usually I have anywhere from three to five journals or Post-it pads with me at all times—each a different size, from a small and slender one that is the size of a credit card and fits inside my wallet to my largest journal, which is about the size of the meaty palm of my hand. I often wear a jacket with a lot of pockets, which is like wearing a secret well-stocked office. I have two fountain pens (one blue and one red). They clip into my left jacket pocket with two unlined three-by-five note cards (unlined is best for drawing). I have a narrow journal in my right jacket pocket. I also like to keep a packet of Post-it notes in my inside jacket pocket. In case of emergencies (jacket stolen by a rival writer), I even keep a skinny "spare" journal in the back pocket of my jeans.

Once I'm loaded up with my writing tools I'm like an old-time gunslinger and I'm ready to step out into my world—the city of Boston, where I live—or anywhere I travel across the United States and around the globe.

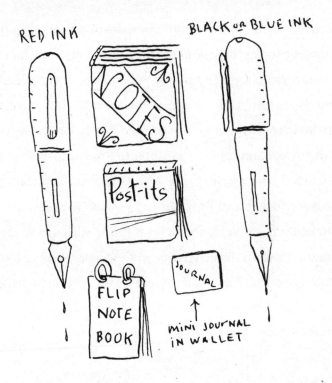

RED INK

BLACK or BLUE INK

NOTES

Post-its

FLIP NOTE BOOK

JOURNAL

↑
MINI JOURNAL
IN WALLET

Some portion of this journal equipment is always with me, and if my Writing Radar goes off, I can jot down an idea or observation so I don't forget it.

I've tried keeping a journal on a cell phone or on my laptop, but I never liked it nearly as much as writing by hand in an actual notebook. If you have a cell phone, you can capture physical details with your camera or quickly dictate notes to yourself. This can be helpful for recording bits and pieces of material—but, again, I prefer a journal because when I am writing I am more aware of using the language to capture the action and emotions. Plus, *all* my senses seem alerted—a photo can capture visual details, and video can add movement and sound, but through the written word I can more accurately re-create the things I feel and smell and even taste. And you can't ruin a journal completely. Once I was in a rowboat on the Amazon River and dropped my journal in the water. I plucked it out quickly (before a piranha nipped me). But when I dropped my cell phone in the airplane toilet I just waved goodbye—and later wrote about it in my journal.

4

Turning On and Fine-Tuning Your Writing Radar

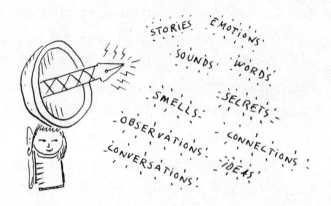

As a writer with a pen and journal in your pocket, you need a certain writerly *attitude* as you walk down the street—a kind of stealthy, snoopy, slinky, shifty, sinister, and silent confidence. This eyes-wide-open attitude activates your Writing Radar.

For instance, when I walk down the street I am sniffing the air; my eyes are looking left and right, up and down; and my ears are on full alert for private conversations, music, ambulance sirens, and vicious dogs. I am searching for interesting visual details (green-haired girl with matching green-haired dog on a leash), snippets of clever dialogue ("My favorite perfume is new-car smell"), unusual behavior (a man dressed as a giant talking book on the library steps), unexpected events (not paying attention and getting clobbered by a police horse as I cross the street), and all manner of descriptions of the life that is richly swirling around me at all times. Not only are my senses paying attention to the outside *physical* world, but I am paying equal attention to my *inside* world. What am I *thinking* as I walk down the street? What am I *feeling*? What am I *imagining*?

All good writers realize that when you complete a story, about half of the story takes place in the outside world (for example: the time I broke my brother's arm, or that day when my dog was eaten by an alligator, or when my crazy neighbor rode his bike off the roof). The other half of the story takes place inside the characters (my guilt for breaking my brother's arm, my sadness at losing my dog, my pained amazement when my neighbor leaped safely off his bike in midair only to slam face-first into a pipe organ cactus).

As a writer, what you strive to achieve is this: When a reader settles into one of your stories they not only imagine the entire filmic action of the story just as you have written it but also feel all the inner human emotions and sensations that make each well-rounded work of literature your unique creation.

So sharp writers must develop a subtle skill—it's not a fancy show-off skill and it doesn't look like anything important, because you don't want it to attract unwanted attention. It's an old-time skill used by the very earliest writers, and it is useful to this day. It's the subtle skill of *being a good listener*, or what I like to call *being a good snoop*. Being a good snoop means that you quietly develop a kind of *antenna* for overhearing sharp stories that take place throughout your day. That's how you fine-tune your Writing Radar.

Snooping, in turn, takes a special skill called *keeping your mouth shut* because you are not the talker! You are the patient listener, and when you sit back and relax with

your ears on full alert you'll notice that people are telling you stories all the time.

But how do you judge the raw story material you are listening to? How do you know if it's good or bad, if it's worth writing down or not? What do you keep and what do you cross out?

The answer to all these questions is simple: If what you hear is interesting to *you*, and if it captures *your* attention, and if *you* want to know more, then you've got a winner. So when you overhear something that tugs on your ear, take some rapid notes in your sneaky journal. These bits and pieces are the raw material that you can later craft into a well-rounded story.

Remember, as the creator, you get to choose the stories *you* love, and you get to polish them into literary jewels. All day long, your turned-on Writing Radar will feed you *the good stuff* to write about.

5

Story Hunting and Gathering

go get 'em!

CAVEMAN STORYTELLER

It's one thing to *talk* about turning on and fine-tuning your Writing Radar to find raw material for the stories you want to tell, and another thing to see it in action. So pretend I'm a kid and let me take you to my old house in Fort Lauderdale, Florida, as my special guest. Let's say it's a Friday night. You can sit next to me as an invisible kid friend at my dining room table and politely listen (or snoop) for yourself to some of the family conversations that took place when I was young.

In my house the dining room table was a storytelling hot spot where I gathered some of my best material as a kid, and perhaps listening to my family will remind you of some of the good stuff you already know from listening to your own family.

My mother was a genius at getting stories started at dinnertime. She used a simple yet effective tactic to coax a story right out of you. After everyone had served themselves and paused to be thankful for the food on their plates, she would wisely point toward one of us (me; my younger brother, Pete; my older sister, Betsy; or my father) and in a hypnotic voice say, "Tell me about your day."

And then magically a story would begin to unfold from whoever was talking.

Well, one night as we gathered at the dinner table, my father had a grin on his face that was rocking up and down like a canoe in choppy water. He had that bug-eyed I've-got-a-great-story look. He was always pulling pranks on people, and I could see he was revving up to tell us something extra-juicy.

"Honey," my mother said as she turned toward him, "how was your—"

"My day was *insane!*" Dad burst out, and slapped his

hand down on the table so hard the salt and pepper shakers hopped up and rolled over. "I pulled a good one today," he said proudly. "In fact, this may be my best gag ever!"

He scooted his chair back and stood up so he could use his whole body to illustrate the story. "See this?" he asked, and pointed to his belt buckle.

"See what?" remarked my sister, Betsy, who was not easily impressed. "It's just your ugly belt buckle."

"Look at it closely," he encouraged. "Something special is missing."

We all leaned forward to get a better view.

"It's missing the fancy buckle cover," Betsy said.

"Exactly!" Dad exclaimed. "There used to be that Spanish piece of eight glued to the clasp!"

"Pizza for eight?" my brother, Pete, asked, but no one paid attention to him.

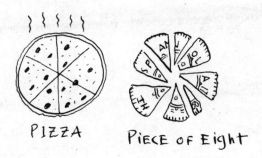

PIZZA   PIECE OF EIGHT

"Was the piece of eight real?" I asked.

"Are you kidding?" Dad shot back. "I won it at the Elks Club raffle. It would *never* be real—it's a worthless piece of fake junk probably made out of a crushed beer can."

"So where is it?" Betsy asked.

"Well, you know the creek we are excavating for the Florida Parks Department?" Dad said.

We all knew about Whiskey Creek because of a surfing champion who was also a famous Florida jewel thief known as Murf the Surf. He had once gone up to New York City and stolen the egg-sized Star of India sapphire from the American Museum of Natural History. He got caught for that heist and the police recovered the gem.

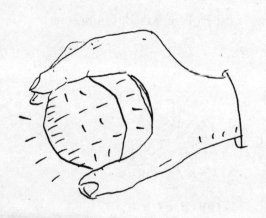

When Murf the Surf got out of jail he returned to Florida and kept thieving. He was arrested a few times, but the police never found all the stolen goods he had stashed in a secret hiding place. Now the state wanted Whiskey Creek searched because there was a rumor that Murf had buried the unfound loot somewhere under the creek bed.

The rumor attracted amateur treasure hunters who sloshed up and down the shallow creek while digging holes and chasing away birds, killing fish, and crushing plants.

The construction company Dad worked for got the job of dredging the creek for any sign of stolen gems and money, and a ranger from the Florida Parks Department had to be on-site all the time just in case some treasure really did turn up.

"Shoveling wet sand is boring," Dad said. "So I thought I'd have a little fun and entertain the workers who were sifting the sand through a wire mesh filter. So I pried the fake piece of eight off my belt buckle with some pliers, sneakily dropped it in the shallow water right where they were sifting, and then just played innocent as I walked off. About an hour later I hear this one worker hootin' and hollerin' that he'd discovered some *real* pirate treasure."

"Oh dear," Mom said quietly. She could see what was coming.

"It was hysterical," Dad continued, beaming widely.

"I mean, this guy thought he had hit the lottery. Then the whole gang starts digging in the sand and looking for treasure."

Dad pulled a cigarette and matchbox from his shirt pocket and lit a smoke. He took a big puff and flicked the ashes into the cup of his open hand. "Of course, all that hubbub drew the park ranger who was overseeing the work. He took one look at the fake piece of eight and his eyes about popped out.

" 'Give me that!' he says, and snatches it. Any idiot could see it wasn't silver, but I guess this guy wasn't too sharp. Next thing he does is shut down the job and rope the area off. Says the creek bed is now an archaeological site and has to be historically examined."

"Did you think to say something to the ranger about what you did?" Mom asked quietly.

"It wouldn't be a joke if *I* pointed it out," Dad replied. "It will only be a joke when *they* figure out that *they* went ape over a fake piece of eight and made monkeys of themselves. Get it? That's when everyone will have a good laugh." Then he giggled while picturing that hysterical moment.

"Really?" Mom questioned. "Do you think the ranger might be embarrassed once he figures out you made him look like a fool?"

"Nah," Dad replied, and waved off her remark. "He has a sense of humor." Then, having said that, he took a final puff on his cigarette and jabbed the glowing red tip into his uneaten clump of mashed potatoes.

Writing Tip.

Snappy dialogue helps reveal character. Plus, there is nothing like showing a bad habit (putting out a cigarette in food) to get a reader's attention!

"That's disgusting," scolded Mom. "Don't put your cigarette out on your dinner plate—that's probably something men in prison do, like Murf the Surf."

"Maybe Murf escaped," declared my sister. "Because I noticed my diary is missing *again* from my room—and I have a pretty good idea of who the thieving Murf the Surf is around here."

She had gotten a diary from my mom, and was a big show-off writing in it.

"Don't look at me," I said with a shrug. "I'm sure there is nothing as valuable as a piece of eight in your diary."

She propped her elbows on the table and glared at me as if she were a poisonous snake. "If I catch the thief with the goods, I'll kill him. No mer-ceee!" she vowed.

Suddenly Pete shouted, "And I'm so *frustrated* I could *kill* myself!" He began to pull on his hair as if it were on fire. "I've been watering my penny-seed plant six times a day for a week, and not even a weed has grown there." He scowled at me. "You gave me a dud seed," he said in a pout, and crossed his arms as he slouched down into his chair.

My mother looked at me with a disapproving glance. The week before, I had given him a single penny for his last-minute birthday gift and told him to plant it and water it and it would grow into a bush covered with pennies. He didn't believe me until I read him *The Carrot Seed* by Ruth Krauss, illustrated by Crockett Johnson. In the book a boy plants a carrot seed and waters it and waters it and no one believes it will grow, but with all his heart the boy believes it will. Days of watering go by, and then one day a huge carrot grows and everyone is surprised. But the boy isn't surprised because he has always believed in himself.

But Pete was right: the penny seed was a dud. At the moment, however, I needed to change the subject because I was the dud brother who gave him the penny.

"Don't lose hope," I quickly said to Pete, and patted him on the shoulder. "Keep watering!"

Then swiftly I turned away from Pete and looked my mom in the eye. "I have a great idea on how to make new friends in the neighborhood," I said.

"How? Pay them?" my sister cracked, and made a doubtful face.

I ignored her. "After helping the librarian when school was out, I was walking up our driveway when I saw a bunch of *huge* cockroaches out in the yard and I had one of my genius moments. I ran into the house and got a Hot Wheels car, some Scotch tape, and a spool of thread.

I grabbed a roach, taped it to the top of the car, and then I used the thread to make a collar and leash.

"Oh, Roachie the Roach"

"I went outside and started strutting down the sidewalk pulling my leash and roach friend behind me. I even named him Roachie the Roach and made up a little song about him."

I sang the song for my family:

"Oh, Roachie the Roach,
The Hot Wheels ra-cer,
Zipping 'round the track,
Fast as a tra-cer.
When he takes first place,
The crowd cheers, 'Yay-sir!'"

My brother laughed at my song like it was the funniest

thing he'd ever heard. My sister screwed her face up and said she thought the song was more likely to make enemies than friends.

"Well, you know the Bad Deal from next door?" I asked.

Everyone nodded. "Bad Deal" was our nickname for the troubled older kid from the Deal family, who lived next to us.

"He was out in his front yard sharpening a knife on a rock he had spit on. I kept singing my song, and when I got close to him I asked him if he wanted to meet my pet roach.

"Right away his face got all puffy and red like boiled meat, and he slid the spitty knife into the waist of his pants. He gave me a psychotic-killer look and marched over, and when he spied Roachie taped onto the car and the thread in my hand, he just snarled, 'What are you? Some kind of roach-loving freak?'

"And then he pushed me out of his way and lifted his big black combat boot and crunched down on my little roach friend.

"'Hey, that was my pet!' I said, stepping toward him.

"'Freak,' he repeated, and reached for his knife. 'Get lost before you are next!'

"I guess I didn't move fast enough because then he crunched his big boot down on my foot, which really hurt—it still hurts—and so do my feelings because I was beginning to like my little roach pet."

"Well," Mom said hesitantly, "that was quite an episode."

She didn't appreciate the cuddly pet qualities of roaches as much as I did. Nobody did.

"And," she continued, "would you believe I had a run-in with his father today?"

"The Big Deal himself?" Dad asked.

"Yes. The bank had me working at a teller window today when the Big Deal came in just before closing time. He gave me a twenty-dollar bill and asked for change.

"'Small bills,' he said in that slurpy voice of his. 'All singles.'

"I was in a hurry to close up my window, so I made

The "Deal" Family

change quickly. It wasn't until he was gone that I gave the twenty a good look, and that's when I suspected that he gave me a counterfeit bill."

"Why'd you think that?" I asked.

"Because Andrew Jackson looked like my uncle Jackson," she replied, "and the face of my uncle Jackson would be printed on a WANTED poster before being printed on a twenty-dollar bill."

"What'd you do next?" Pete asked.

"I took the twenty to the manager, and he's sending it to the Secret Service to be tested. If it is phony, they might arrest the Big Deal."

"I love a happy ending," Dad remarked, while picking his teeth with a matchstick.

"But it could have been an honest mistake," Mom said, trying to be fair.

And then in the next second she *clap-clapped* her hands together.

"Time to clear the table," she said briskly, and picked up two serving plates.

6

The Writing Journal in Action

and then Dad pulled the piece of eight off his belt buckle and tossed it into the creek!

Dinner may have been over, but not my curiosity. The bits and pieces of dinner stories were prowling around my imagination like beginnings hunting for endings. Would Dad get into trouble for disrupting work? Would Betsy catch whoever had run off with her diary? (I hoped not!) Would Pete's penny seed have a miraculous transformation and grow? And would Mom get into trouble because of the Big Deal and his funny money?

After I helped clear the table I went right to my

bedroom, got out my journal and favorite fountain pen, and started writing down all the good stuff I remembered before I forgot it.

Why I Use Fountain Pens

The fountain pen is the greatest writing tool ever invented. It's fast and fancy and makes my handwriting look like George Washington's. You can find inexpensive fountain pens at your local stationery or office supply store. Some models use ink cartridges, and others require refilling from bottles of ink. The fountain pen creates the best curvy lines for drawing, and it always  leaks a little, so I have ink on my fingers—the stains of a real professional writer! Plus, if anyone tries to snatch my journal I can whip out my pen and stab them in the hand!

Not every dinner at my house served up a tasty seven-course story collection like this one, but because I was a good listener I often walked away with a *story starter*: a single detail, a snippet of clever dialogue, or some unbelievable action I could write down in my journal and perhaps use in building one of my own stories.

Of course, each night at the dining room table, everyone would add to their stories as if they were delivering another chapter in a book. And, like you, I was always eager to find out what happened next so I could write it down.

Unfortunately, you didn't eat dinner at my house any other night, so here are the short versions of how the family stories worked out:

- For Dad, after a few days of work stoppage at Whiskey Creek he broke down and told the park ranger about his little piece-of-eight joke. As Mom suspected, the park ranger was not amused, and neither was Dad's boss. Soon Dad was transferred to repairing a leaky sewer system at the county prison.
- As for Pete and his penny tree, I felt guilty about the dud seed, so eventually I planted a whole hibiscus bush in the backyard and taped pennies to the branches. When Pete discovered it he was blown away. He had honestly believed with his whole heart that planting a penny would result in a penny tree, and now he knew it was true.
- As for my roachy run-in, that same week the Bad Deal was arrested for taking a neighbor's car for a joyride and was sent to juvie.
- Finally, the twenty-dollar bill the Big Deal passed to my mom at the bank turned out

to be phony, but the Big Deal claimed it had been given to him as change at a gas station and he had just innocently passed it along. No one could prove he knew he was committing a crime, so he was not arrested. But we never believed him.

So this was the typical back-and-forth conversation at our dining room table, with bits and pieces of stories passed around like meat and potatoes. Everyone got a serving. Maybe it's the same at the dining room table at your house. If so, always remember to chew with your mouth closed because capturing a good story is the result of being a good listener—not just a *talker*.

And if you have been a good reader, you have realized that one of my dinner-table stories is not finished—the story about Betsy's missing diary. I've saved that story for its own chapter because it was my tough older sister who gave me my first lesson about journal writing. It was a lesson I learned the *hard* way. The *painful* way. The *sister* way.

So let me tell you the whole story about my sister's missing diary and me. I have the perfect title for it.

7

"I'll Kill You," Said My Sister

My sister, Betsy, was by far the smartest one in the family. She had straight A's on her report card. I had straight C's. She sang beautifully. I sang so poorly in chorus class that my music teacher actually taped my lips together. (Then I sounded like a kazoo.)

My sister was a skillful artist who could draw anything she gazed at. For me, all my trees looked like telephone poles wearing bad wigs, my misshapen people staggered across the page as if they had just survived a tragic car accident, and my animals were stitched together from random pieces of other animals.

But I did have one natural talent, and that talent was to simply copy everything my sister did. I was a genius at being a copycat.

For instance, she spent most of her time reading stacks and stacks of good library books. When she finished one and set it down, I picked it up and read it through.

When she had a new favorite song, I was singing it badly day and night.

When she had a new favorite food, I ate a ton of it.

When she had a new favorite friend, that person had to be my friend, too.

Naturally, when she got a diary as a gift from my mother and began to write, I wanted one, too. My mother refused, but I had a plan.

Mom was in the kitchen expecting a long-distance phone call from an old friend. She didn't want to be bothered, so it was the perfect time to ask her for a diary.

I was sure she would say yes just to get rid of me, but when I asked again she instantly replied, "No. I already told you—no diary for you." She wagged her finger in front of my flat face like a windshield wiper sweeping away any hope of my getting a diary.

My shoulders slumped. "Why?" I asked.

She looked up at the kitchen clock. Her friend was late, and the only time she had to talk was when Pete took a nap. "Because you'll never write in it," she stated firmly. "It will be a *waste* of good money. It will sit on your bedside table or on a shelf and just become dusty *clutter*, like all your other abandoned projects I paid for."

"No it won't," I protested. "I'll write in it. I promise."

"Never make a promise you can't keep," she cautioned. "Now, don't pester me. Go do something useful. Get a pair of pliers and pull the ticks off your mangy dog like you promised to do yesterday."

"Can I play dentist with Pete and pull out his teeth?" I suggested. Pete was a biter.

"If you wake that baby up, I will use pliers on *your* teeth!"

The phone suddenly rang, but when Mom picked up the receiver the line was dead.

"Ugh!" she said impatiently. "Just forget the pliers. Go mow the lawn. But don't run over your foot and nearly hack it off like the last time."

She exaggerated. The mower blade had cut clean across my sneaker and only sliced a sliver of skin off the top of my foot.

"It missed the bones," I reminded her. "And the *S*-shaped scab on my foot is cool-looking—like I'm Superman."

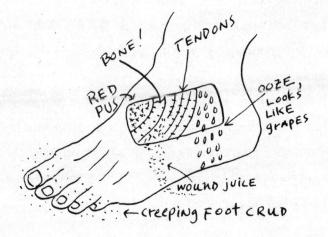

"Actually, the *S* stands for *Stupid-man*," she shot back. "Go mow the lawn, because I'm one second from telling you to go jump in front of a freight train."

I had already survived doing that, but kept it a secret. Our house was close to a train depot. An old train had been parked there for so long that the wheels were rusted to the tracks. It wasn't going anywhere, so I thought it would be a good idea to practice diving across the tracks just in case I had to escape from a child killer or a rabid dog or an angry sister. I sprinted up the side of the gravel train bed. When I reached the tracks I dove headfirst toward the other side, but I belly flopped across the second steel rail. The train would have sliced me in half. The rails are a lot farther apart than you might think, but I couldn't share that lesson with my mother.

Just then the phone rang again. "Get a move on!" Mom snapped, and jerked her thumb toward the door. "Vamoose!"

I did. I went to my older sister's room to get some writing advice on keeping a diary even though Mom wouldn't give me one. That turned out to be a mistake. As usual, I just got some writing *abuse*.

I knocked on her door.

"Don't come in," Betsy hollered right back. "I'm not dressed properly."

That was an old excuse. I went in anyway.

She was fully dressed and staring into a hand mirror while curling her eyelashes. "What are you here for?" she asked harshly.

"You have a diary, but Mom won't get me one," I said. "Maybe you can change Mom's mind for me."

"I'm on Mom's side," she shot back. "Your brain is like a burned-out lightbulb that can't be changed. Besides, you haven't done anything interesting enough to write about."

"Well, since you are so interesting," I quickly replied, "why don't you let me read your diary so I can get a lesson on what to write? I'm kinda stuck about how to get good ideas."

"No way," she shot back. "My diary is private. It's brilliant and locked, and I keep the key around my neck." She fished a string up from around her neck and showed me the small silver key that looked like it was carved out of a dime.

"Okay," I said to her, with my

shoulders slumping in defeat. "You're probably right. I'm totally boring."

But as I walked away I realized that that small key had to fit into a small lock—a lock that could be easily picked open with a stiff wire. That thought filled me with wicked hope.

A week later Betsy spent the night with a school friend. I went into her bedroom and opened the underwear drawer where she kept her diary. I grabbed it and dashed back to my room. I tried to pick the lock with paper clips, fishhooks, sewing needles, eyeglass screwdrivers, bits and pieces of wire—but nothing worked. *Nothing!*

I've always been patient, but my patience was wearing out. My failure to pick the lock was driving me crazy, and with each failed attempt I became even more frantic to read all of my sister's shrewd observations about her friends.

What did she write about our family? I bet it was insightful. I especially wanted to know her private boyfriend secrets. She said she despised the Bad Deal creep next door, but I figured her journal would tell me otherwise.

She was smarter than I was, and I imagined her journal

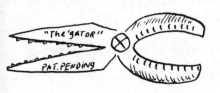

"The 'GATOR"

PAT. PENDING

was like a book-sized honeycomb just dripping with sweet, sticky creative ideas that I would lap up and in an instant I'd transform into a superhero writer.

Finally, my patience wore out and in a crazed moment I removed the pair of wire cutters from my back pocket. I gritted my teeth. There was no turning back. I snipped open the lock. I knew she would know it was me, but I couldn't help myself. I had lost all self-control.

I grabbed the diary and went into my closet and dropped to the floor. I turned on my flashlight. I pulled the lock aside and flipped open the cover to page one.

In block print it read, "KEEP OUT, YOU BORING MORON!"

I grinned. *Too late for that,* I sang to myself.

The anticipation of reading her brilliant words made my hands shake. I began to drool. I just knew this was going to be one of the most memorable, mind-blowing moments of my life. This was going to open the door to a whole new world for me—a smarter world than I had ever lived in.

On page two I excitedly read her first entry: "It's a

beautiful sunny day. I'm very happy. Life is good. My friends are nice."

The rest of the page was blank, except for pink pencil drawings of wildly happy dancing flowers.

That wasn't interesting. I quickly flipped the page and read the next day's entry: "It's another beautiful day. I'm really joyful. Life is grand. My friends are sweet." She had drawn a row of her friends' angelic faces.

Ugh, I thought, and flipped to the next page.

"Hooray! It's yet another beautiful day," it read.

It wasn't beautiful for me.

I had a bad feeling I wasn't going to find what I was looking for: the good stuff, the really juicy story material.

I wanted the *action*!

The *emotions*!

The *insights*!

The *descriptions*!

The *deep thinking*!

And all those *personal secrets*!

Quickly I flipped through the remaining pages. Each one was as sappy as the next.

As I now suspected, it was all mind-numbingly dull and it lowered my IQ to read it. I went from drooling in satisfaction to drooling from being stupefied.

I felt tricked. Betsy's journal was the dreary menu of a pathetically bland life without any spice. There was nothing nourishing in there. It was like she was a genius at being an echo chamber of sweetness.

Sure, I was a jerk for trying to find out her private secrets—but I was far more disappointed that she didn't capture any interesting *truths*! There was nothing to read that would make me stop wide-eyed at the end of a sentence and mutter to myself, *That is so true!* Or, *I always felt that way but didn't know how to say it with such power!* Or, *That is brilliantly poetic, I wish I had written it first!*

Not one of her sentences had opened a door into a creative world that would transform the way I saw life. I always thought she was like Alice, who in *Alice's Adventures in Wonderland* follows the White Rabbit down the rabbit hole and discovers a fabulous world of anarchy and exotic characters. But Betsy must have followed the *Blah* Rabbit and got her head stuck in a bucket.

And worse, there was not one word about me in her journal, and I had been certain she would have written about me because I was so annoying to her. But no, I didn't exist in her journal, which is the same thing as saying I didn't exist at all. To her, I was a waste of ink.

And now I had another problem. She would know I

had cut the lock off. That was obvious. I didn't have the guts to return her diary to her room, so I hid it. I crawled into the back of my closet and shoved the journal into an old coat pocket. Then I closed the door on myself.

As I squatted there in the dark like a quivering coward, I finally had that great mind-blowing moment of insight I was looking for—and it was *painful*. Instead of reading her diary and gaining confidence in my writing, I realized it was my own insecurity that had led me astray. I only read her journal because deep inside myself I didn't think I could write anything original on my own. I didn't *trust and believe in myself*, which meant I was hollow on the inside except for my sudden guilt and remorse and self-loathing for reading her diary. Even in the darkness of my own closet I lowered my head in shame.

And then panic clutched my heart as I felt the broken lock in my hand. I knew my sister was going to kill me.

I spent most of the weekend trying to glue the lock back together and touching it up with gray paint so it would look perfect again. I figured she hadn't noticed that her diary was missing because she hadn't said anything.

But at Sunday dinner, she announced that her diary had vanished. She gave me a suspicious look, and I knew I was soon going to suffer.

After dinner, when she was taking a shower, I quickly put the diary back where I had found it. Maybe if I was lucky, the moment she touched the lock and it fell apart she would think she had broken it.

But it didn't happen that way. After her shower she returned to her room. A minute later she must have looked in her underwear drawer and found her diary. The lock must have fallen apart in her hand, because then I heard her she-wolf howl: "Jaaaack! You are dead!"

She came sprinting down the hallway with bright, rabid-red eyes.

I bounded off the living room couch and dove toward the front door.

Like a missile, she intercepted me in midair and pinned me down onto the floor. "I'll kill you," said my sister.

"Don't be angry," I quickly blurted out. "There was nothing in there anyway. It was so *boring.*"

I thought my comment would wound her pride and weaken her resolve to kill me. Instead she raised her fist and stunned me. Maybe she knocked me out with one punch because the next thing I knew she was gone and I was flat on my back and groggy.

I tried to stand up, but my legs were numb and lifeless. I undulated like a worm across the living room and then crawled on my hands and knees down the hall.

When I finally limped into my bedroom I found it ransacked as if Murf the Surf had been looking for the crown jewels. Betsy must have been searching for *my* diary, but I was in luck—I didn't have one yet. I was going to save up and get one, though, because I had learned my lesson. There was *no cheating* when it came to writing. There were *no shortcuts*. There was *no copying*. And most of all, I would have to get over my greatest fear—that everything I wrote would be boring. I was going to have to get a diary and write what I thought was interesting. Only then could I know if what I wrote was any good. Being successful was up to me, and I was up to the task.

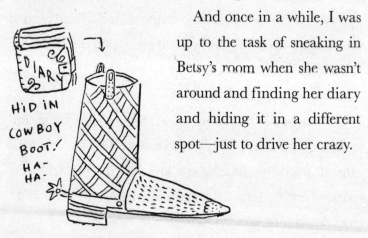

HID IN
COWBOY
BOOT!
HA-
HA-

And once in a while, I was up to the task of sneaking in Betsy's room when she wasn't around and finding her diary and hiding it in a different spot—just to drive her crazy.

8

The Oath

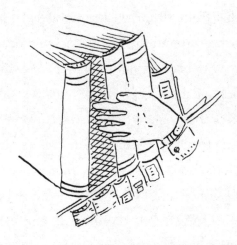

After my run-in with Betsy, I restarted my journal mission—and this time I did it the right way. No funny business.

Here is what I did, *and what I'm about to tell you is exactly what I want you to do.*

I made a deal with myself and took an oath that would change my entire life.

After school I was in the library helping the librarian, Mrs. Hammer, reshelve books. She had a last name that made her sound tough, and she was. She had been fired from two other schools for "abusive behavior." I wasn't sure if that meant abuse of kids or abuse of books or both, but I knew that when she hit a kid with a book both kid and book suffered. But she also had a big heart and protected me from all the wicked kids who never read but just sharked around the library looking for trouble. So I was happy to help her out whenever she asked.

Well, I had a book cart full of returns I was reshelving. You can probably guess that the *G* section was my favorite reshelving territory. That day I did what I always did. As I pushed my book cart I ran my fingers across the spines of the *G* authors until I came to my future book slot, the one with GALDONE on one side and GEORGE on the other. I could imagine my book, with my last name, GANTOS, fitting snugly on the shelf between those two authors. Of course I didn't have a book with my name and title on it to reshelve between GALDONE and GEORGE, so I shoved in the next best thing—I stuck my hand between those books and wiggled it back and forth until I opened up a dark, vacant slot. As I stood there a powerful feeling came over me, and I lowered my head.

My father had always told me that a man's handshake

is as good as his word. And so with my hand pressed between those books I whispered an oath and promised myself that I would begin to write a book—no matter how hard the task—and *I'd trust and believe in myself* and *wouldn't be a quitter* and my book would someday fit exactly where my hand was now.

I placed my other hand over my heart. "I give my word of honor," I said gravely, and then slowly shook hands with that empty slot.

Once I removed my hand I quickly finished up my library work. I waved goodbye to Mrs. Hammer and marched out the library door and down the street to the stationery store while thinking deeply about my oath and what I had to do to keep it.

I had saved up my chore money, and at the store I bought an inexpensive new journal. It was a small black book that was an artist's sketchbook. There was no lock on it. The pages were unlined and unnumbered for

This is the only writing oath you'll ever need:
I will trust and believe in myself.

drawing, and the binding was strong, which was necessary because I dropped my books a lot. The black book came with no directions or rules. Whatever I wrote inside of it, good or bad, was up to me. The sharp tip of my pen was now the boss of every word in the dictionary, and it felt good to be the boss of something as amazingly powerful as the entire English language. All I had to do was to tell each word where to line up. That sounded easy enough, but I suspected it wasn't easy. Words always have a mind of their own.

As it turned out, my writing oath became one of the most important promises I have ever made to myself—and it was a promise I kept. So I want you to go to your library and find exactly where your future book with your name on it will fit on the shelf. Then I want you to shove your hand into that slot and promise yourself that you, too, will write a book and that someday it will be on the library shelf for some reader to check out and take great pleasure in reading.

Yes, I want you to do that. Not just for me, but for yourself. *Now, do it!*

9

Blank Slate

Of course, when I was standing there in the
library swearing my solemn oath, it was easy to close my
eyes and imagine a beautiful book with my name boldly
printed on it. Still, I was old enough then to understand
that a bit of steady effort—even very hard work—was
going to have to go into the writing of a book, and my
promise gave me the backbone to keep on going.

I took a penknife and on the spine of my new journal
carefully carved my last name: GANTOS. For a title I

just carved out **BLACK BOOK** on the cover. I left it at that. The book was just like me: nothing fancy on the outside to attract attention, but on the inside it was *all me*!

My imagination was already on fire. The journal was going to be one wild universe of my orbiting, crazy, reckless, tilted, dangerous thoughts. It was going to be juicy with blood and guts, love and sadness, and poetry and power. My black book was going to be my brilliant lunatic twin.

I took that black book everywhere. But despite my oath and repeated promises, the pages remained pretty empty. Once in a while I would hear some great stuff at the dinner table and scribble down bits and pieces. But I could never seem to think of things on my own to write down. It just seemed that I had a mind full of great ideas, but when I opened the journal to write them down the white pages turned my mind into a blank white slate.

I couldn't figure out what was wrong with me. I felt smart. I knew I was creative. I had story ideas that seemed funny or important, but it was the *act* of writing them down that was the sticking point. Picking up the pen and putting the nib on the paper seemed about as dangerous and forbidding as sticking a fork into an electrical outlet.

And when I did finally get a few words written, every story opener seemed more absurd than the last.

One sentence never led to another. I could write weird ideas, but they never turned into a story. There was no beginning, middle, or end—just a bunch of dead-end sentences.

After a while my will to write began to abandon me. I got to the point that if I dared to write one word in my journal, even in pencil, I felt I'd mess up that perfect sheet of paper with my imperfect, scratchy thoughts. The pure

Five Story Openers from My First Journals That Went Nowhere

One morning I found a dried-up thumb in my cereal and on the thumbnail was written: RETURN TO SENDER.

Cloud shadows on the wall at night looked like the secret rash I hid from my mother.

I stepped into a deep fur-lined hole and expected to enter an exciting imaginary world, but it turned out to just be a deep fur-lined hole. After an hour I was sweaty and bored and climbed out.

I'm such a backward mess that I have a better chance at telling the truth when I lie.

My mother sniffed my armpit and barked like a dog. The dog sniffed my armpit and miraculously began to talk like my mother. "Take a bath," he said.

white paper was like some kind of brain bleach, and the more I stared at the page the less colorful my ideas became, until after hours of staring my unwritten ideas slowly faded from my mind.

I sat staring into the open book as if I had opened a door into an empty room. I knew it wasn't the book's fault. It was my fault.

Clearly I did not have what it took to write a story. I wasn't *smart* enough. I wasn't *imaginative* enough. I wasn't *tough and disciplined* enough. I gave up and hit rock bottom. I had nowhere to turn, except back to the library, and so I trudged all the way there while imagining what it was that I had to do.

I was going to drop to my knees in front of the slot between GALDONE and GEORGE and confess that I had tried to write a book but had failed—failed miserably at the first step in the process.

I couldn't even get *one* good sentence written down on a page.

I was going to go back on my oath and stop believing in myself.

I was going to snap all my pens in half.

I was going to become a different self—the nonwriting self I would regret for the rest of my dreary life.

But then, at the last moment, something magical did happen: I was rescued by an inspirational book.

Even though I was feeling like a loser, my Reading Radar was still working! As I was heading disgracefully for the *G* author section I passed by the *F* author section and a book caught my eye.

The title was *Harriet the Spy* and the author was Louise Fitzhugh. The word *Spy* in the title appealed to me, so I stopped and pulled the book from the shelf. I flipped it open and sat on the carpet reading a few pages and it wasn't long before the book took me over and rescued me.

Harriet gave me the greatest tips for writing.

What she did was walk around her neighborhood

boldly spying and snooping on her friends and neighbors and listening to their conversations and writing it all down—she wrote the good stuff and the bad stuff, but it was all the *real* stuff.

I loved that idea. I liked spying on other people like a boy detective. My mother had told me that intentionally overhearing other people's conversations was rude, and I should never do it. Now I made another oath, and I wrote it down at the beginning of my black book: "When it comes to writing I should do just the opposite of what my mother tells me to do."

I checked out *Harriet the Spy* and went directly home. I finished it that night. I was so inspired I don't think I slept a wink.

After school the next day I got my journal and a large piece of paper and put them in my bicycle basket. Then, with my confidence renewed, I pushed off and went hunting for action!

10

Story Maps

READY TO ROLL

I slowly rode around my block and on the paper I drew a rough spy map of my neighborhood.

Right away my Writing Radar was pulsing with incoming thoughts. It was alerting me that I was onto something good, because when I drew on the paper my ideas didn't fade away or seem hopeless. They seemed *inspired*!

With each house I drew, I could *see* where all the nutty people lived and where all the crazy stuff happened—the *action*.

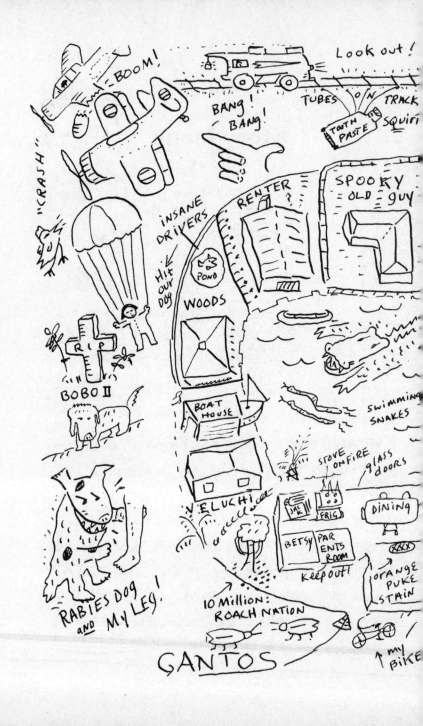

The map included a mean dog, and beat-up cars, a burned spot on the road where an airplane had crashed, grumpy old people who yelled at us, the place where I broke my brother's arm (it happened three different times), the swimming pool where Dizzy Deal (Bad Deal's younger brother) knocked a dent in his head, and portraits of me, Pete, and Betsy. Everything I looked at became brighter and more exciting and seemed to tell a great story. The drawings anchored my thoughts.

Soon I was sitting under a palm tree, making notes in my journal about everything I knew about my neighborhood, and the words were running wildly across the page. And then it hit me—*bam!*—that it was as if the map of my neighborhood was a giant dinner table, and everyone who lived on my block had a story to tell.

All I had to do was be like my mom and coax a story out of each drawing by asking, "How was your day? Tell me what happened."

My mom knew a great writing secret. Learning how to ask the right question of a person, place, or thing is the best way to get a story started.

It was amazing to me that once I began to fill in the map I discovered that I was right at the center of the action and all the good stuff to write about was swirling around me. And what better place to be as a writer than at the *very center* of your own universe, where you are the most important character. And to start a story all you have to do is look at your map and say:

> *"What happened there?"*
> *"What do I think happened?"*
> *"What do I want to have happen?"*
> *"What happened next? And next?"*

Each answer connected one thought to the next, and before long the sentences were connected like train cars rolling down a track.

My belief in myself was surging, and my oath was more alive than ever. The black book in my hand with maps and story-starter ideas was the proof I needed that I was going in the right direction.

Still, I didn't know as much as I needed to about my neighbors in order to write whole stories about them. That would come later, once I spent more time spying on them and figuring out what kind of people they were on the inside. But for now there were some people I knew inside and outside: *my own family.*

So I went home and drew a second map of my

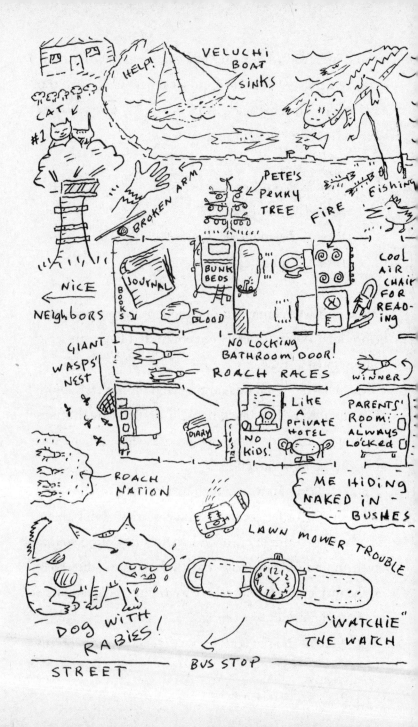

home—a full house-and-yard map. I took a big piece of paper and drew out all the rooms (I didn't forget the dining room table), the yard, the penny tree, our pets, and more portraits of me, my brother, and my sister.

This map was full of *action*. I drew where things broke, where we played games, where blood was spilled, where more bones were broken, where I kept my roach collection, where the hot dogs exploded, what stories we told each other during dinner, where the wasps lived, where the birthday cake caught fire, where I hit my head on the sliding glass door, where I pulled a wart off my foot with pliers, where I hid naked in the bushes, where I vomited on the wall and left a smelly stain, and where we danced and had fun playing golf inside the house.

Soon it seemed that every room in my house had a story, or two or three. And from listening to all our dinner-table stories, I knew that the action almost always was in the middle of the story.

So when I looked at the drawing of the smelly stain on the living room wall where I vomited up my mother's spaghetti, I knew that vomiting was the action!

I then knew I was going to have to find a beginning that would explain what I did that caused me to vomit on the wall. After that I'd find the ending that would show what happened to me after I had vomited on the wall.

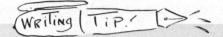

If I looked at the drawing of the kitchen stove, I remembered how my sister set our house on fire trying to make french fries. The fire was in the middle of the story. The beginning was how the fire started. The end was about cleaning up after the fire.

My Writing Radar was pinpointing the action, and I was mostly fitting the action into the middle. Here is one of my first attempts to write a more complete story from my journal. It's not great, but I was getting there.

The Hot Dogs Are Exploding!

Every time I look at the grill in the backyard I remember the time my dad gave me the big responsibility of cooking the hot dogs for dinner. I put the hot dogs on the blazing hot fire and they started swelling up like hot-dog balloons. Why were they doing that? I was confused. Then I was scared because they started to explode. *Bang! Bang!* I was getting splattered with hot dog chunks and grease.

In fear I screamed out, "Dad, Dad, somebody is shooting our hot dogs!"

My dad came running out with a baseball bat, but soon he figured out that my imagination had gotten the better of me. Nobody was shooting our hot dogs. I had forgotten to take the invisible plastic wrappers off the hot dogs and they swelled up in the heat and exploded.

The End

This hot-dog story has a lot of action in it. And it has some good details. Clearly it is an improvement on just writing "One night the hot dogs blew up." Still, I needed more than just action. I needed a better beginning and a better ending. And I needed some emotion, too.

With practice, I knew I could connect each improved part of a story into a whole flowing story—and that is just what I was after!

11

Action *and* Emotion

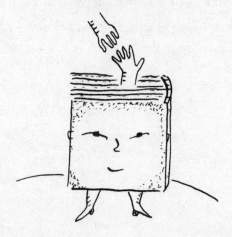

When you are a good reader you naturally love the great action in a story. It keeps the pages turning. But you want something more, too. Something deeper. You want the emotions to be equally as powerful and interesting as the action. You want to feel what the characters feel. It is the human feelings that create a handshake between the reader and the character.

In fact, for a good story you need a balance between the action in the world around you and the emotions you feel in the world within you. The actions that take place in the story cause emotions to spring up inside the characters. And the reverse is also true. Emotions in the characters cause them to spring into action.

I knew this, in a vague sort of way. My Writing Radar was guiding me. So, even after locating the story *action* on the house map, I knew the stories were only half baked. They were missing the other half—the human *emotions* that turn an okay story into a great story. The reader has to feel all the emotions that the characters feel so that he or she can understand the *whole* story.

Spy Guy

Sometimes I go outside at night and hide behind a tree and listen to people talk as they drift by. Or I sit in a café and eavesdrop on the conversations around me. I write it all down in my journal. A lot of it is about romance. *Hate* is a word that everyone says the same way. On the other hand, everyone has their own special way of saying *love*.

Action is easy to locate because you can *see* action. But emotion requires asking a few questions of the action.

For instance: On my map I drew my sleeping dog, Bobo, in the backyard, because one day an alligator crawled out of the canal and ate him. That was action! But as I thought about that event, I asked myself, *How did you feel about it?* I had felt afraid, and guilty for not saving my dog. And sad.

I drew a wasps' nest on the side of the house because

my sister gave me a stick and told me, "Hit the nest and they'll all fly next door and sting our creepy neighbors." That didn't work! I smacked their nest and they all came after me. I ran for the back sliding glass door with my eyes closed and hit the door and knocked myself out. (That was good action, but how did I feel? Tricked by my sister again. Angry. Stupid.)

The front yard bushes I drew on the map reminded me of when I got locked naked outside the house and had to hide behind the bushes until my dad came home from work. (Ugh. *How did you feel about that?* I felt humiliated. My dad and sister thought it was funny. My mother was embarrassed. The neighbors thought I was weird.)

These are all good action moments and surefire story starters, and the moment the emotion is added they get so much better!

So after you draw your action map, I want you to sit down with your map and take a good look at it. For every action on the map I want you to ask yourself, *Okay, what is the strongest emotion I had when that action happened?* As a result, your map will end up looking like my new map, which lists both the action and the strongest emotional word that links up with that action.

To give you an example, here is another little story I wrote in my early journal. It's not long, but you can see I'm trying to capture a better balance between the action and emotion as I also organize the story so that it has a clear beginning, middle, and end.

The Cool-Air Chair

We don't have air-conditioning in our house and it is hot in Florida. I hate feeling sweaty. So one day when my mom left to go shopping I got a genius idea and sneakily pulled a chair up to the open refrigerator door. I took a paperback out of my pocket and sat on the chair and propped my sneakers up on an inside shelf. I felt brilliant. The cool air blew over my legs and across my chest and face as I read in total air-conditioned bliss.

Once I invented this luxurious way to read I would pull up a chair in front of the refrigerator each time she left the house to go shopping.

But one day I was reading a good book and lost track of time. Suddenly I heard Mom's car pull up the drive-way. Yikes! I jumped into action and rapidly put the chair back where it belonged. I closed the refrigerator door, and tossed my book down the hall. By the time Mom entered the house with a bag of groceries I was standing on the other side of the kitchen with an innocent look glued onto my face. I thought I was so super sneaky.

And then my mother opened the refrigerator door. She didn't say anything, but something seemed wrong to her. When she is quiet I know she is thinking. The longer she stood there the harder my heart began to pound.

Finally, she turned and called out, "Jack! Come look into the refrigerator and explain this to me!"

I dashed over to the refrigerator. "What, Mom?" I asked in my innocent voice. "What may I help you with?"

She pointed to the top shelf and asked, "Why are your steaming sneakers in the refrigerator?"

"COOL-AIR CHAIR
AND BOOK STORAGE!"

I had stupidly kicked them off when I was reading and forgot to take them out.

I shrugged. "Weird stuff happens," is all I could think to say as I looked down at my bare feet. My mother followed my gaze. She reached down and gripped my foot. It was as cold as the refrigerator.

"Confess," she ordered, and narrowed her eyes at me.

I told her what I had been doing. I thought she would kill me, but she just shook her head back and forth and smiled.

"Never let your father catch you doing this," she warned me. "He's been complaining that the electric bill has suddenly climbed sky-high."

"I have been reading a lot," I said proudly, then I gave her a hug.

"Next time," she whispered, "pull up an extra chair for me."

I knew why she was letting me off the hook. She was a reader, too.

The End

In this story you get to know the characters better than in the exploding-hot-dog story. Plus, there is more of an emotional ending when my mom and I share a special *feeling* for each other because we are both readers.

I was also proud of this story because it has a clear beginning (me setting up and enjoying my cool-air chair), middle (me losing track of time while reading and Mom coming home), and end (me thinking I'm going to get in trouble, then Mom surprising me by not being mad). It was a big improvement because I used a good balance of action and emotion. My writing practice was paying off.

12

Power!

I was never good at chemistry. However, once I figured out how to mix action with emotion I realized what power they would create, and I wrote this equation down in my journal:

ACTION + EMOTION = CHANGE IN THE CHARACTER

What this means is essential for all writers!

When you write a good story about a character (yourself or someone else), there will obviously be action and emotion. But the best writers know that action and emotion are *forces* in the story that cause the characters to change from the beginning of the story to the end.

The *power* of stories is experienced within the reader. This means that when your characters change by experiencing something new, feeling something new, or understanding something new, then they influence the reader to change, too.

A writer has the ingenious power to change the world. One reader at a time.

But to come up with the right story mixture to sway your reader, you need to always look for the *action* and the *emotion*.

After you set up your house map with both actions and emotions, I want you to make two helpful vocabulary lists at the front of your journal. I find that sometimes a single word can remind me of a great story that I may have overlooked.

The first list of words may inspire you to think about where some interesting *action* took place that you can add to your map, and later use for story material.

Key Words That Lead to Ideas
for Action in a Story

Brothers

Sisters

Parents

Public humiliation

Best friends

Nutty neighbors

Sleepovers

Singing

Movies

Dumb stuff

Secrets

Sports

Eating

Vacations

Grandparents

Reading

Getting sick

Triumphs

Lying

School

Disasters

It ALMOST Killed ME!

I FOUND A HUNDred BUCKS!

Chores
Finding stuff
The wrong friend
Scars
Creepy things
Music
Fire
Pets
Religion
Cleaning your room
Being grounded
Swimming
Gardening and yard work
Crying
Laughing
Broken bones
Writing
Phobias

(Copy this list into your journal and
add ten more of your own words)

To go along with this list of story-starter words that
might lead to action is a list of emotion-packed words. An
emotion might match up with an action you have drawn

on your map, or it may inspire you to remember an action you forgot.

A strong emotion is always caused by something that happened—some *action* that took place or is about to take place. A strong emotion inspires you to remember the story that caused such a powerful feeling.

Key Words That Lead to Ideas for Emotion in a Story

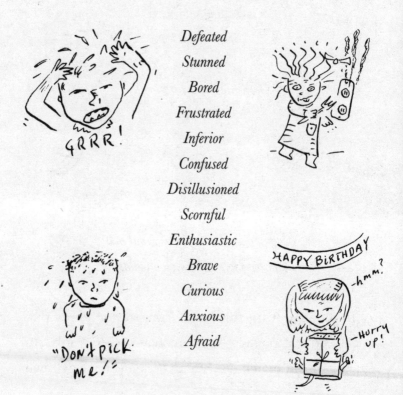

Defeated
Stunned
Bored
Frustrated
Inferior
Confused
Disillusioned
Scornful
Enthusiastic
Brave
Curious
Anxious
Afraid

Neglected
Hopeless
Grumpy
Worried
Awkward
Insulted
Cheerful
Proud
Content
Amused
Tender
Helpless
Dread
Powerless
Bitter
Spiteful
Relaxed
Loved
Trusting
Fearful
Quiet
Humiliated
Pity

Accomplished

Jealous

Triumphant

*(Copy this list into your journal
and add ten more words)*

13

Good Habits Lead to Great Inspiration

Action and emotion are a great team, and every story needs them to turn an okay story into a great story. There is also another important team—*inspiration* and *good writing habits*—and they have to exist within the heart and soul of a writer if that writer is to be a great writer.

Inspiration is what you feel as a writer—what you get excited about when your Writing Radar spots something incredibly brilliant to write about. But unless you follow up on your moments of creative inspiration and write them down (good writing habits), you will be damaging your Writing Radar. In fact, it will be like unplugging your Writing Radar and tossing it in the trash, and no writer wants that.

Those exciting moments of great inspiration are what motivate me to write. So don't be satisfied with only saying to yourself, *This is a great idea,* because if you don't write it down it won't be a great idea. It will be a great lost idea—a *dead* idea. This is why inspiration and good writing habits are a team.

Good Writing Habits

1. Find a quiet space at home or in the library.
2. Have a pen you like to use, or a pencil with an eraser.

3. Open your journal and read your last writing entry.
4. Set writing goals: ten or fifteen minutes per day for new material, every day if possible.
5. Before closing your journal, make a few quick notes on what action or emotions might happen next. This will give you a head start for your next writing session.

For example, here is a true story of how my Writing Radar spotted the real kid that inspired me to write *Joey Pigza Swallowed the Key* and how I captured the moment of *inspiration* through my *good writing habits*.

Picture this: I was on a two-week speaking tour of schools in Pennsylvania. I was close to the end of the tour, and a bit weary from teaching all day and then traveling to another town at night and the next day teaching at another school.

But my Writing Radar was not tired when I visited a fifth-grade class at Buchanan Elementary in Lancaster,

Pennsylvania. I was in a typical square classroom. The teacher's big wooden desk was in the back corner, and the welded together unibody student desks were in their usual rows—all except for one desk. The bug-eyed boy at that desk had scooted his desk away from the others until he was about two feet in front of me. He didn't sit in his chair but knelt on the seat, and then with one leg he hooked his foot into the back ladder-slats of his chair. He slowly began to spin, and then spin some more, and then spin faster and faster until he was like a helicopter blade spinning 360s, and each time his face swung by mine he grinned wildly.

You can imagine that this was a little distracting for me, the speaker, and for the students, but the teacher paid no attention to him because she was used to it.

So I began to speak and I had just delivered the first half of a sentence when suddenly the kid swooped by and finished the second half of the sentence. I started another sentence and he swung by with his eyes bulging out and his arms gyrating, and he once again finished my sentence—using the *exact* words I would have used to finish it.

Before long it was as if there were only two of us in the class—me and him. I would start an outrageous sentence and he would finish it in a brilliant way.

When I said, "I was running with scissors," he quickly added, "And then I cut off her nose!"

When I said, "I stuck my finger in the pencil sharpener," he hollered, "And I twisted off my fingernail!"

This back-and-forth banter went on for about ten minutes. The other kids watched us like we were a weird dog-and-pony circus act. The teacher stared at us and wondered when our little act would blow up. She didn't have to wait long.

After a few more spins the kid's wildly happy expression began to turn into a worried, nervous look, and as he spun in circles his eyes were no longer focused on me. They were now glued to his teacher. She was paying attention to another child when suddenly he couldn't hold back from blurting out the problem that was frustrating him. He shouted, "Teacher! Teacher! Help! I forgot to take my *meds*!"

She suddenly looked up at him with a jolt of alarm on her face and pointed toward the classroom door, and that kid somehow unhooked his twirling foot from the back of the chair and shot like a whistling boy-rocket out of his seat, past me, and through the doorway, where he landed on his feet and began to zigzag down the hallway punching the lockers—*bam! bam! bam!* Between the punches he cawed out like a panicky crow, "Nurse! Nurse! Wait for me! Joey Pigza [not his real name] is coming to get his special meds!"

I never saw that kid again. But my Writing Radar was pulsing off the charts and signaling at me: "Write that down!" I was so inspired by what I had just seen I wanted to stop speaking and grab my sneaky back-pocket journal and sit at Joey Pigza's desk and write down all the action and all the surging emotions that had just captured me. But I had all those other students staring at me, and so I had to finish my talk.

After that class I right away had another class. And another. Finally, at the end of the school day, I was put into a car and driven to the next town, where after dark I checked into a scary truck-stop motel room.

I was exhausted. I sat on the edge of the bed and

leaned forward with my face in my hands and my eyes closed. But inside of me that remarkable kid was still spinning around and dancing a jig down the hallway while yelling, "Teacher! Teacher! Help! I forgot to take my meds!"

I knew he was special. I felt deeply what he felt, and I cared for him right away. I knew he was a good kid—but maybe he was also a misunderstood kid. Whatever he was—the good, the bad, the special, the out-of-control—I knew it was up to me to get his story down on paper.

So as tired as I was, I sat up and got my journal and a pen. I began to write, and I wrote word after word as if I were the one punching the lockers—*bam! bam! bam!*—and I kept writing, imagining all sorts of crazy things Joey might do.

At the end of the trip, when I was sitting in the airport waiting to catch my flight home, another kid just like Joey Pigza came bouncing by at full speed. He was like a human spring that had popped out of a giant toy.

His mother hollered at him from down the hallway, "Get back here this minute!"

And without missing one of his springing, prancing

leaps through the air, he threw his head back like a rooster and crowed, "Can I get back to you on that?"

My Writing Radar nearly knocked me over! I lunged for my book bag and pulled out my journal and wrote down, "Can I get back to you on that?"

When you get a good idea write it down or you will lose it. In other words, don't put money in a pocket with a hole in it.

That airport kid was a genius, and the moment of inspiration he gave me was the special tagline of dialogue that captured Joey Pigza's unique voice: "Can I get back to you on that?" Once again, my Writing Radar was fully turned on and I was *inspired* and *I wrote it down*. I wasn't about to let something that juicy get away from me.

These days I can't go to a school and speak to kids without a student prancing by me while yelling out, "Can I get back to you on that?" Or they raise their hands after a presentation and when I call on them they gleefully yell out, "Can I get back to you on that?"

The lesson here, of course, is that if I didn't write down what had inspired me I may have lost that great moment when Joey flew out of his desk and down the hall. I may have let it fade away. And then that great tagline of "Can I get back to you on that?" wouldn't have meant anything to me. And I never would have written five Joey Pigza books—books that I think contain some of my best writing.

Not a day goes by that I don't think of Joey, and believe me, my Writing Radar is always on and I'm always on the hunt for inspiration.

So keep your Writing Radar on full alert because when inspiration strikes it may be the most important first step to grabbing your journal and fulfilling the oath you made—the oath that you will work hard to achieve your dream of seeing a book on a shelf with your name running down the spine. (That is the true meaning of *spine-tingling*!)

You want that feeling. I know you do.

Which is why I have even more to teach you.

Now, turn the page!

14

Story Structure and Story Elements

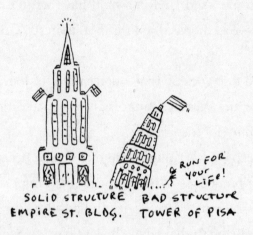

SOLID STRUCTURE   BAD STRUCTURE
EMPIRE ST. BLDG.   TOWER OF PISA

So we have covered *action* and *emotion* (the physical and emotional world found in every good story).

Just as important, we covered *inspiration* and *good writing habits* (two dedicated abilities that every writer needs).

Now we have to talk about another team of writing partners: the *story structure* and the *story elements*.

Structure is what we all know as the beginning, middle,

and end of a story, and the *story elements* are the handful of basic storytelling pieces that fit inside the structure of a story.

Basic Story Structure with Storytelling Elements

In the BEGINNING we have:
- Characters and the voice/point of view of the person telling the story (the narrator).
- Setting (where the story takes place—the setting may change as the story advances).
- Problem and theme (what the story is about).

In the MIDDLE we have:
- Lots of rising physical action (what the characters are doing) and emotional action (what the characters are feeling) that show off the characters and highlight the problem and theme (what the story is about).
- The problem is always revealed through the

physical and emotional action in the middle of the story.

- The rising physical action and emotional action build up to a crisis.
- The crisis can be a physical crisis, an emotional crisis, or both.

In the END we have:

- A resolution (a solution to the problem found in the beginning of the story).
- A double ending: both a physical ending (what happens to the character) and an emotional ending (how the character feels and changes) to complete the story and highlight the theme.

Don't be a slackeR! Copy This story structure into YouR journal.
— Jack Gantos

As you can see, the structure of a story is basic: just a simple beginning, middle, and end.

The story comes alive inside the structure and is created by using commonsense *storytelling elements*: characters, setting, problem/theme, rising physical and emotional action, physical and emotional crisis, resolution/solution to the problems, and a double ending—both the physical ending and the emotional ending, which will highlight the change in the main character.

These elements are easy to use and are helpful tools for when you are organizing your story, or if you get a little lost while writing. The elements will always point you in the proper direction.

Corduroy Bear by Don Treeman

BEGINNING · MIDDLE · END

Problem! · Action! · Solution!

"I don't have a button. My pants are sagging. No one will buy me. I'm lonely." · "I looked everywhere for a button." · "I got a button and made a friend. Now my pants stay up and I'm not lonely."

For instance, when you are stuck while writing, just ask yourself, *What do I do next?* Then look at your list of story elements. Maybe you need to introduce a clear problem. Or perhaps it is time for the big action of the crisis? Or maybe the action is over and you need to solve the problem?

Some people might think that structure gets in the way of creativity, but I find this to be entirely untrue. Structure helps you organize and shape your ideas. Plus, when you look into great literature you will always find it is made of the combination of purposeful structure and brilliant creativity.

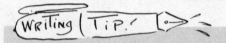

WRITING TIP.

The reader never pays attention to your structure because he or she will be entirely mesmerized by your captivating characters, seamlessly flowing action, and powerful ending. Only you, the writer and creator, are paying attention to your smartly organized structure.

Here is another way (a concrete way) to think of the structure and the storytelling elements.

My father built buildings for a living and often, as we drove down the street together, he would stop the car in front of a magnificent new building and admire the sharp design of it. He would call the outside of the building the *structure*. Then he'd park the car and talk our way inside the building, where he would show me what he called the *elements*.

We'd walk through the building from the basement all the way up to the roof. Floor by floor, he'd point out what held the building together—the concrete foundation with iron reinforcing bars in it, the steel frame and beams, the thick floor joists to carry the weight of each floor, the solid elevator shaft that is the unbending spine up the middle, the well-proportioned walls and windows, all the way to the perfectly pitched roof. He knew buildings so well that his eyes X-rayed them so he could see the *structure* and all the material *elements* that combined to make such a perfect building.

A story is built much the same way. It has a structure and elements within the structure that combine to hold the story together and keep it from falling into a heap of mismatched pieces. When a story I'm working on has a broken structure, I find that the elements just don't line up properly to form a perfect beginning, middle, and end. So always pay attention to the teamwork between the *structure* and the *elements* of your story.

15

Putting My Oath
to the Test

_"GOOD LUCK,"
I whispered, and
ran my finger
down its spine.

After months of writing in my black book I
finally filled it with all the wildest stories I had located on
my *action* and *emotion* maps.

Of course I did not know anything about using *story
structure* to organize the *story elements* when I was sitting in
my bedroom writing in my black book. I wrote pretty much
the same way I talked at the dining room table, which was
from the first-person point of view (*I* said, *I* did, *I* felt, *I* saw).
I generally knew a story had a beginning, middle, and

end—but that was about it. Still, it was enough to get me started.

I kept my journal a secret project. Sure, I was afraid my sister would read it and make fun of me. But more than that, it was a project I wanted to do on my own just to see if I actually would complete my oath.

I wrote a lot at night in my room, and once I filled all the pages in my black book I knew there was one person I had to show it to because I needed her help. I brought it to the school library one morning and sat down with my tough-as-nails school librarian, Mrs. Hammer, and this is what I blurted out: "I wrote a book full of stories and I need a library book call number to stick on the spine so maybe some kid will check it out and read it."

Mrs. Hammer looked taken by surprise. "Really?" she asked, and pointed at me with a ruler. "*You* wrote a book?"

I pulled the black book out of a little velvet bag that the Bad Deal had left in his trash (I was doing a little deep snooping). I reached forward and put my book into Mrs. Hammer's hands.

She weighed it like holding a piece of red meat. "Feels like you packed a lot of words in here," she remarked.

"Everything," I said, "including the kitchen sink."

Then I leaned forward and whispered, "Even stories I overheard from snooping outside the teachers' lounge."

She laughed out loud. "You are a nut," she cackled. "But the kind of nut I like."

I grinned. When a person you respect calls you a nut, it's a compliment.

Then she looked me in the eye. "Did you write any curse words in this book?"

"I forgot to," I said.

It was her turn to grin.

"Did you say anything derogatory about the principal?" she asked. "I don't want to lose my job."

"You are safe," I replied. "I have a great story about the principal, but I am saving it for after I leave this school."

"Good choice," she declared. "Okay. I'll help."

She typed up a fake library book label and pasted it on the bottom of the spine:

FICTION
GANTOS

I glued a card pocket on the inside back cover and slipped a Date Due card inside.

It was cool-looking. And it felt incredible to finally hold my own book in my hands. But I was paralyzed. I just stood there, frozen, and stared at the Black Book.

"Now go ahead," Mrs. Hammer insisted, and waved her hand toward the *G* section. "Put it on the shelf."

"I'm a little afraid," I confessed.

"What's the worst that can happen?" she asked. Then she answered her own question: "Someone might read it and think you are insane!"

"I'm afraid of people laughing at me," I said quietly.

"Nonsense. Now do what you have to do," she ordered. "If you chicken out, the Hammer will come down on you!" She raised her menacing ruler over her head.

I took a deep breath, turned, and marched out of her office with determination. I had known exactly where my book should go for a long, long time and this was no time to lose faith in myself. In a moment I stood looking at the dark gap between GALDONE and GEORGE.

"I'm back," I whispered. "I made an oath and now I'm fulfilling it."

Then I reached forward and slipped my book right

between those two authors' books. It fit perfectly in the shadowy space between them, just as my hand had fit there when I took my oath to write a book. It was a promise to myself I had kept. Nothing could take that away from me. It was as if I had carved the book out of stone.

"Good luck," I whispered as I ran my finger down its spine, and then I walked away.

It was the bravest thing I had ever done. I held my head up high. But as I walked to class slowly, step by step, I began to have second thoughts. My palms were sweaty. I kept licking my lips.

In class that day I was antsy. My mood swings were like tidal waves crashing on the shore and then receding. One moment I was proud of myself, and the next minute I thought I was the weirdest kid at the school. Whenever a kid even glanced at me I turned away. I feared everyone could read my mind and know what madness I was up to.

All morning I kept peeking up at the clock and the instant the lunch bell rang I flew out of the room and down the hall. I sprinted right past the cafeteria and into the library and down the aisle to where I had placed my book. It was still there!

My hand was shaking as I reached for it. "Have courage," I whispered to myself. "Keep your head up. Don't be a coward now, or you will regret it for the rest of your life. Be strong and walk away with some dignity." I withdrew my hand, but it was shaking.

For the next few days I would pass my book in the library and each time I secretly winked at it, as if we shared a private joke. Then a week went by, and it was still there. Then two weeks passed. It didn't move. GEORGE was checked out, but not GANTOS. GALDONE was sought after, but not *Jack's Black Book*. I would be lying if I didn't say I was disappointed—even dejected.

Once more I thought of pulling my book from the shelf and burning it, but I knew I would despise myself for giving up. I would feel like a quitter, and nothing could feel worse than that. Plus, I had made an oath to honor my promise, so I kept waiting. But it was killing me.

Then one morning I showed up and it was *gone*! GALDONE was back, and so was GEORGE, but GANTOS had vanished! I was so thrilled I did a little Snoopy happy dance. And then I didn't say a word to anyone—not even Mrs. Hammer. It felt good to keep it a secret while I imagined some kid reading it. I hoped they liked it—especially because it was all about me and I had put my heart and soul into the words and stories.

I crossed my fingers that the reader would bring it back and turn it in to the library and not pass it around to the teachers who I *had* written about. It probably would have been a wise idea not to have written about them in a book I put in the library. My mother always advised, "Some things are better kept to yourself."

And now, dear Reader, I'm sorry to do this to you, but for a short while I must leave you in a state of suspense as you wait to find out what happened to *Jack's Black Book* on the library shelf.

WRITING TIP.

It's always good to create a little suspense in a story and make the reader sit up and say:

But what happened Next?

Now I want to show you how strong your Writing Radar is getting by telling you one of my favorite stories, one that I wrote especially for you.

Enjoy reading it, but keep in mind the story structure (beginning, middle, end) and the storytelling elements (characters, setting, problem, rising action, crisis, resolution, physical and emotional ending). The story will give you a clear picture of how all the pieces come together. Afterward, I'll break down all the story pieces so you can compare your thoughts to mine.

16

The Follower

"MY PAL, "DIZZY DEAL"

My mother said he was trouble the first time
I met him, but I liked him right away. He said his name was
Dizzy Deal and he had just been catapulted across his yard
like a human cannonball and landed with a *thud* in ours.

A moment before that happened my mother and I
were in the kitchen unpacking moving boxes. That was
when we heard that first *whoosh* of the catapult and Dizzy
hollering through the air, "Aiyeeeee!"

That was followed by the *thud*, and his soulful moan.

We looked out the kitchen window and saw that he was in our yard and kind of crumpled up on his back like a crash-test dummy. At first he wasn't moving, but slowly he began to unhinge his arms and legs like a stunned crab. Mom and I dashed outside, and by the time we stood over him he was moaning and blinking as he came back to life—or back from the dead.

"Who are you?" Mom asked. "Where'd you come from?" She looked up in the air as if he had fallen out of an airplane.

"Dizzy," he slowly wheezed. "Dizzy Deal. I live next door."

"We live here now," I said, and stuck out my hand to help him up. "We're your new neighbors."

He did not reach for my hand because he was in a lot of pain, and here's why. His much older psychotic brother, who I soon nicknamed Bad Deal, had made him climb to the very top of a flexible Australian pine tree with a rope between his teeth. Then he tied one end of the rope to the top of the tree, and Bad Deal tied the other end to the winch on his rusty old Jeep. He winched the tip of the tree all the way down so that it made the tree a big coiled spring, and then Dizzy Deal held on like a koala bear while Bad Deal counted down and then cut the rope with a machete. Dizzy was launched from the human catapult like the stones the Romans flung at the Vandals.

"Well, are you okay?" I asked Dizzy.

He slowly turned over onto his hands and knees and vomited something dark that looked like frog skin with foam on top.

"Yeah," he said.

He shuddered. "I've had worse."

My mother was not at all sympathetic. She pointed at him as if he were a garden pest. "He's a flying heap of trouble," she said to me. Then she said to Dizzy, "If you have to hurt yourself, please do it in your own yard."

He winced as he nodded in agreement to what she said, and then I helped him up onto his feet and he staggered off looking as dizzy as his name.

A few minutes later Mom and I were back in the kitchen when we heard:

Whoosh!

"Aiyeeeee!"

Thud!

"Ugh!"

He was back. This time we stayed inside the house and he managed to crawl away on his own.

That evening Mom was chopping onions in the kitchen

and I was looking out the window to see if there was any action going on next door.

"Something is messed up with those kids," Mom said. "Something's wrong in their heads."

"Something must be wrong with Jack, too," she thought.

The onions were making her cry, but she might have been crying because she suspected there was something wrong in my head, too. I was different from Dizzy Deal, but we had one thing in common: from the first moment I saw him in pain and anguish, it occurred to me that I wanted to be in pain and anguish, too. My mind was funny that way.

My mother must have read my mind, but she kept her thoughts to herself until later. That evening she came into my room when I was filling my dresser with clothes. "This is just a *friendly* warning," she said, and reached out to hold my head between her hands as if she were speaking directly into a needy part of my brain. "But if I ever catch you playing with that crazy Dizzy kid, or over at his house, you will be in big trouble."

"Why?" I asked, and pulled my head away. "He's a neighbor, and I think he's about my age. We might go to the same school. He could be a friend."

"You have a habit of making the wrong friends," she said, referring to some of my old dangerous friends who had led me astray. "Kids like him are a danger to themselves," she continued, "and they can be a danger to others—like you."

I got some courage up and replied, "But that's what interests me about him."

She pointed a red finger at my chest. "Let me make myself perfectly clear," she said bluntly. "You are a *follower*, not a *leader*. You are putty in the wrong hands. Don't get me wrong. You're a nice kid, but you are most definitely a *follower*."

I sort of knew this was true, but I didn't want to admit

it to her. Plus, a little part of me still wanted to believe that I was strong, that I was my own man and a great leader, and that I was not headed for trouble.

Within a week I was Dizzy Deal's man, which was pretty wild because he was Bad Deal's man, which made me low man on the totem pole—or pine tree.

The first time Bad Deal launched me from the catapult I hit a car. It was an old Mercury Cougar parked in

their backyard. It sat on its belly like a cat crouching to catch a bird. I hit the roof, which was a steel trampoline. It dented down, and then popped up with such force I went springing awkwardly off the top. As I was in the air, I kept thinking, *When you hit the ground, roll and tumble and it won't hurt so much*. This is what I had learned from watching *Sunshine State Roller Derby* on TV. It was my favorite show and very violent, but the players always avoided massive debilitating and life-threatening injuries as long as they rolled and tumbled across the wooden track or over the rails and onto the rows of metal folding chairs.

So as I flew through the air I stared down at the grassy yard and planned my clever descent. I hit the ground with my outstretched arms, but instead of bouncing as if my hands were shock absorbers, I collapsed onto the ground like a piece of space junk.

I dislocated the fingers on my right hand, squashed the side of my face, and sprained my right shoulder. I limped home hunched over like Quasimodo and went straight to my room to catch my breath. A little later I was barking in pain from cracking my knuckles back in place on my bad hand. I was so afraid my mother would see my bruised face that I borrowed my sister's makeup and powdered my bruise. At dinner I couldn't use my right arm. It hung limply by my side like an elephant's trunk, except for when it twitched unexpectedly as if I were trying to swat flies. I must have pinched a nerve on contact with the ground, and now it was spastic. *Perhaps I'll be this way for life,* I thought. I figured I had a pretty grim future as I ate with my unskilled left hand while food kept tumbling off my fork and down my chin and shirt and onto my lap.

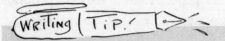

If you can make the reader wince and laugh
at the same time, that's twice as good.

"What's wrong with your arm?" my mother asked as my spastic arm jerked about.

"Nothing," I mumbled.

"We'll see about that," she said, and swiftly came around to my right side while the rest of the family watched in curiosity. She grabbed my wrist and pulled it straight back as if it were the starter handle on a lawn-mower engine. Something deep inside my shoulder went *pop!*

"Arghhh," I said with a sigh. The relief from the pain was heavenly and I slowly slumped down into my seat.

"You are as dumb as a post," my mother declared. "I'm warning you—don't play with that kid! He'll lead you to your death."

But I couldn't help myself. I had already started down that path to self-destruction and there was no turning back.

The next day my arm felt pretty darn good, and as soon as my mother went into the bathroom with a magazine I dashed over to Dizzy's house. His brother, Bad, had rigged up a deadly new torture device by using a model train transformer. He ran copper leads from the transformer to chicken wire he had duct-taped onto the wooden seat of an old chair. It looked totally primitive and harmful, and when he turned it up to full power the electricity crackled through the wires and the duct tape smoked and smelled like hair on fire.

For a moment I thought my mother was right. I shouldn't be so attracted to what was painful. But my follower instincts were far stronger than her warning.

"Don't be a chicken," Bad said demonically, and pointed at my rear end. "Take a seat, say a prayer, and meet your maker."

I took a seat and cupped my hands over my kneecaps. When he turned the power dial up, it was torture at its most challenging and sublime. After I had survived a thirty-second blast at half power, Bad wasn't satisfied that I had suffered enough. He made me follow him into the kitchen. He splashed a glass of water onto the back of my pants and had me sit down again.

"Fire in the hole!" he hollered, then turned up the dial. The water conducted the electricity to my bottom. I began to steam, and when he gave me a full charge I shot off the chair and rolled head over heels across the floor.

"Good one," I remarked from the far corner of the room.

"Jack!" I heard my mother calling from our house. "Jack, where are you? Come help me with dinner."

"Gotta go," I said to Bad as I stood up and brushed my bottom off. "But I'll be back for another dose."

"Momma's boy," he sneered, then shoved Dizzy toward the chair, where the melted tape was still sizzling.

As I trotted across their yard I jealously thought I heard Dizzy scream.

At home I dashed straight to my bedroom. I dropped my pants and looked at my naked butt in the mirror. It was criss-crossed with the same chicken-wire pattern that was on the chair.

"Wow," I said, touching the red grid across my tender skin. "Pretty cool."

The next day my mother did the laundry. She came to

me with my undershorts, which were singed with the same wire pattern.

"You don't have to tell me how this happened," she said, sounding worried. "You just have to stop. Whatever drives you to do this self-destructive stuff is a sickness. So I'm grounding you for a while until you start displaying some good sense."

Maybe I was sick. Maybe I was a follower. But I couldn't help myself. I wanted to sneak back for another jolt on the chair. I was just thinking of how to sneak out my bedroom window when I looked over at the Deal house and spotted Dizzy pushing his bike up to the peak of his roof. Their house was only a one-story ranch like ours, but he was still amazingly high up.

Sitting in a lounger by the edge of the pool, Bad Deal was directing Dizzy into position. Soon he was poised to pedal down the slope, fly through the air, and land in his swimming pool, which I thought was quite a distance from the edge of the roof.

"Get a move on!" Bad demanded. "Don't be a cry-baby. You can make it."

Dizzy hesitated. "Are you sure I can make it?" he yelled down.

"Piece of cake," Bad hollered back. "Now, go for the gold!"

"No guts, no glory," I whispered to myself. "Do it!"

Dizzy pedaled as fast as he could and yelled all the way down the roof, and then he was in the air. My vision was blocked by a bush, but what I heard next was all wrong. Instead of a splashing sound there was the sharp, springy metal clang of Dizzy's bike hitting the concrete patio and then clattering around. In a minute Bad was hollering at Dizzy to stop being a sissy and to stand up, and that the dent in his forehead wasn't anything to cry over. I slowly rubbed my hand over my forehead as I glanced in the mirror. *Perhaps a little dent of my own would look good*, I thought.

I got a screwdriver from my closet toolbox and began to unscrew the clips that held the insect screen over my window. Once I got the screen off I was going to slip out the window, grab my bike, and make a dash for the Deal house. But suddenly my mother stepped into my bedroom.

"Cross that kid's name off your list of friends," she said matter-of-factly. "That's an *order*!"

"Is he dead?" I asked.

"The question," she said gravely, "is what kind of *limited* life will he have from this day forward?"

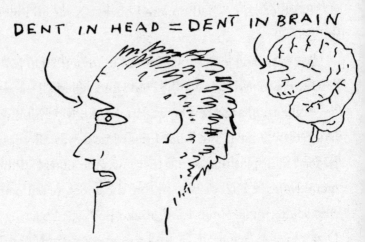

DENT IN HEAD = DENT IN BRAIN

MOM'S Thinking about DIZZY'S HEAD DENT

In the distance I could hear the siren of an ambulance. Soon the paramedics arrived and took Dizzy away.

The next day, after some begging, Mom allowed me to visit Dizzy in the hospital, and later, once the Bad Deal was sent off to a special program for permanently dangerous boys, my mom even allowed me to go over to Dizzy's house a few times. His dent was filling in nicely, and most of his brain functions had returned, though he still wasn't sure how to play checkers and tried to bite one as if it were a cracker. But because he had stopped doing dumb things for Bad, I stopped doing dumb things, too.

Dizzy was a follower just like me. And when you put two followers together nothing really awful happens. Without a dangerous leader, we didn't hurt ourselves or do anything too stupid and moronic. About a month went by before I secretly wished Bad Deal would return home and rescue us from being such helpless losers. I was bored out of my mind.

Then school started and eventually I was busy with homework and I stopped seeing Dizzy as much.

After a few weeks my mother came up to me and put her arm around my shoulder. "I think you've turned a corner," she said warmly. "You stopped playing with that dangerous kid, and now you can make some normal friends."

"Yeah," I said, and smiled sweetly at her as if I were a docile idiot.

But what she didn't know was that I was desperate to meet some dangerous kid at school who would take me under his wing.

It didn't take long.

In gym class we were playing baseball when I spotted

a kid that looked hazardous to my health. There was something crazy about his eyes and the careless way he wildly swung the bat whisker-close to other kids that made me want to meet him.

The next morning my mother was reading the newspaper at breakfast. I was getting ready to leave the house when she held up the paper and said, "Take a look at this *winner*. I bet his mother is hiding her face today."

There was a picture of the crazy-eyed school kid I wanted to meet. He was sitting up in his hospital bed. The caption on the picture was "Kid Goes Ka-Boom!" I read the story. He had made a baseball from gluing together hundreds of paper cap-gun caps and after school was testing it out to see if the gunpowder in the caps would explode. The last thing he remembered was tossing the ball up into the air and taking a big swing at it. He didn't recall much of what happened after that except for a very loud noise. From the picture he looked fine to me. I didn't see a piece of the bat sticking out of his head or anything.

"He goes to your school," Mom remarked. "Do you know him?"

I could tell she was fishing for information. He was just the kind of kid she knew I liked.

I shrugged, and before I could say anything the

doorbell rang. I froze. The doorbell was like a coin toss. I never knew what was waiting for me on the other side. It could be trouble, or worse. My mother was always inviting over her friends' boring kids who wanted to do normal stuff with me.

"Don't just stand there," Mom ordered. "Answer it."

I walked across the living room and opened the door. It was Dizzy. He was holding the newspaper open and pointing to the same story about the hurt kid.

"I think we found what we've been missing," he whispered. And then he smiled slyly. Even his dent smiled in an upward way.

"Let's go buy him a get-well card," I added. "And after school we can go visit him in the hospital."

"Yeah," he said gleefully. "Let's go play follow the leader."

17

Breaking It Down

All right, my Writing Radar led me to the wild story material you just read in the preceding chapter; now let's break this story down into its basic elements.

Characters

My mom, me, Dizzy Deal, the Bad Deal, and the crazy kid at school.

Setting

Begins at my house, and then shifts next door to the Deal house, then to school for a moment, and then back to my house.

Problem

I'm a "follower"—and like to hang out with a "leader" who thinks up dangerous games. My mother wants me to choose better friends.

Action

Starts with the human catapult game, rises to the homemade electric chair. I get grounded but try to escape and ride my bike off the roof, too.

Crisis

Dizzy Deal gets hurt and has to go to the hospital with a deep dent in his head.

Resolution/Solving the Problem

The Bad Deal is sent away. Dizzy and I lose

our leader. My mom tries to protect me from my own tendencies, but I am still drawn to dangerous people.

Double Ending (always use a double ending!)

- Physical ending: Doorbell rings; Dizzy has located a new dangerous leader.
- Emotional ending: I'm gleefully back in business as a follower. I know it's wrong, but I just can't help myself.

You can clearly see that the elements within the structure become a step-by-step guide to lead you through a story from the beginning, to the middle, and then to the end. This is obviously helpful for organizing all the pieces of any story.

There is also another key reason why it is helpful: Because I know the basic structure of a story, when I sit down with my journal and start to put together a story, I can be wildly receptive to *all* the creative thoughts bombarding me at once.

Here is what I mean by that: Often, when writers sit in front of a blank piece of paper, they expect that their first creative thought will be the perfect first sentence of the story, their second creative thought will be the perfect second sentence, their third creative thought will be the perfect third sentence, and so forth, as if each creative thought were somehow lined up neatly in the back of their brain like a long string of dominoes standing on end and all the writer has to do is push the first one over. Then one by one each domino will obediently tip over to form a long, perfectly organized story—and thus the destiny of each domino, like lemmings going off a cliff, will be complete. If writing were like this, it would probably be robotic and dull. Besides, it is totally unrealistic to think that perfect sentences are going to drop to their knees before you like falling dominoes.

And yet some writers are stubborn. I write in the library all day and I look across the room and there is always someone staring at a blank sheet of paper for hours just waiting for that perfect first sentence. While they wait, perhaps fifty good ideas pop into their mind, but they toss them aside like trash because they are stuck waiting for the world's most perfect first sentence. In the meantime, I go home at the end of the day having captured hundreds of good sentences that I can polish up later.

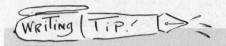

Don't be that writer who waits all day for the perfect first sentence, or you will grow old while learning to hate yourself and writing.

TICK-TOCK
TICK-TOCK
TICK-TOCK
TICK-TOCK

Waiting for the perfect sentence

Here's the kind of writer I want you to be: First, you sit down in front of an open notebook or a blank sheet of paper with a general idea of what you might write about. Most likely, random thoughts are riotously crisscrossing your brain in ways that are wildly wonderful yet wildly confusing.

So where do I begin? you ask yourself. *Where is my first sentence?*

Maybe the first clever thought in your mind is a vision for a brilliant ending. Don't say to yourself, *I can't use that brilliant ending at this time. I'm only at the beginning of the story, and I need a first sentence for a character with a problem.*

If you are a bad writer, the brilliant-ending vision gets tossed in the trash simply because it arrived in your brain out of turn. But you are not that bad writer. You are smart. You take that brilliant-ending idea and you look at your story structure and instantly you know to roughly place that brilliant-ending idea toward the end of your story.

Immediately after you place the brilliant ending toward the bottom of the page, another idea strikes you. Perhaps it is an action scene, and so you know it will go roughly in the middle of your story.

Well, when writing a first draft of a beautiful story, you can just start with making a rough outline—if you know the elements and structure. Then *every random thought* that flashes through your mind can be a *productive* thought. You can sit in front of a blank page fearlessly as ideas pepper you like meteor showers. Your job is to capture each idea no matter when it arrives, and then you place it approximately where it might belong.

By example, let me use a few details from my novel *Dead End in Norvelt*.

When I started that book I knew I needed some action in the beginning that would lead to a problem. I had a few so-so ideas that I was listing, but then out of the blue I had a strong vision of me accidentally firing off my dad's Japanese sniper rifle, which I thought was unloaded. I knew that action was a winner of an idea, one that gives the book a fast start—and a big problem.

When I needed memorable characters I made a list but settled on the unforgettable Miss Volker once I imagined her boiling her own hands in a pot of melted wax at the stove to relieve her arthritis.

Another thought I had was for a distinctive bit of dia-logue that reveals character. Mr. Spizz, who is a gruff old bully, is always hollering at me in the story. So I gave him a catchphrase: "Hey, Gantos boy!" he always growls when he sees me.

When I needed a clever and daring friend, I created Bunny Huffer, whose dad runs the Huffer Funeral Parlor. Once I created Bunny, I decided to make my character in the novel afraid of seeing dead people. Bunny is not afraid of anything, so we have a good friendship (especially because there turn out to be a lot of dead people in Norvelt).

In this way I could bundle like-minded story ideas together. To keep forging ahead, I kept asking myself basic "What happens next?" questions, which are always just variations on my mom's story-starter question at the dining room table: "What did you do today?"

So when Jack first goes to Miss Volker's house and discovers her boiling her hands in a pot on the stove, I asked myself, *What does Miss Volker do and say?*

When Mr. Spizz first spots me in front of my house where the grass hasn't been cut because I've been lazy, I asked myself, *What would Mr. Spizz do and say?*

When Bunny Huffer learns that I'm afraid of seeing a dead body, I asked myself, *What does Bunny do and say?*

As a writer, I knew that with this kind of steady work I

would begin to create well-described thinking and speaking characters (which is a great accomplishment).

If you have an earlier thought that defines a problem (gun firing), you might find a later thought that leads to solving the problem (who put the bullet in my father's sniper rifle?). You learn to quickly gather and write down these raw thoughts in a loose *problem-action-solution* or *beginning-middle-end* structure, which is a bit like an outline. Then once you have a general idea of your characters and the setting and theme/problem and the rest of the elements, you can begin to fill in the action and details.

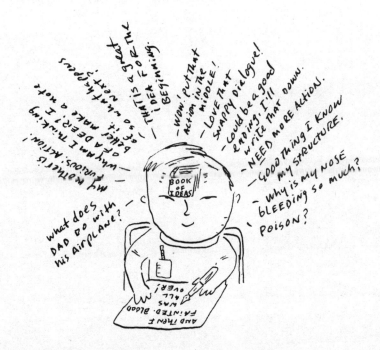

I stress knowing the elements backward and forward inside the structure of a story, because your creative mind is tossing you out-of-order genius ideas all the time and it is your job to seize each idea and ask, *Where can this best be used?*

Please, as I've warned you, do not become the writer who stares at the sheet of paper all day waiting for the perfect opening sentence while ignoring all the other brilliant thoughts that do show up. Be daring. Put your thoughts into words on the page. Only then will you see how to organize your story.

18

My First Reader Teaches
Me a Lesson

Mrs. Hammer

Okay, I've kept you in suspense long enough.
Let me tell you what happened to my story journal after
it disappeared off the library shelf.

After two long weeks of staring at my empty book slot
on the shelf, I thought maybe it was pretty foolish of me
to have put the only copy of *Jack's Black Book* up for grabs.
Whoever checked it out probably didn't think it belonged in the library and instead donated it to a mental

institution that studied the writing of the insane. Or maybe they just wrote *LOSER* all over it before dumping it into the trash. I was feeling pretty ridiculous. The empty gap on the shelf where my book had been now looked like an empty spot left by a missing tooth.

But then it came back! It was a miracle. I was working in the library and Mrs. Hammer came over and handed it to me. She had found it in the book return bin. I quickly flipped to the back, where I had written a note on the last page asking the reader if he or she liked the book. Whoever read it had responded. Eagerly I read:

Whoever wrote this book should SEEK MENTAL HELP! CALL: 1-800-NUT-JOB!

That sounded just like my mother, but I was sure she hadn't checked it out because I had kept my book experiment secret from my family.

I did, however, seek help. But not from a doctor.

I knew I needed professional help—and it wasn't going to come from my sister, either.

The same day the book was returned I stayed behind after English class and timidly showed my black book to my teacher, Mr. Adolino, who had been pretty nice to me all year. It was a risk I had to take. I didn't know anyone else who might help me.

"I'm writing a book," I said. "It's a mess right now. Can you read it and give me some advice?" I held it out to him. "You are the only one I can trust not to laugh at me."

"I wouldn't laugh at you," he replied with a smile as he took the book. "But you are a funny kid, so I hope I laugh at your stories."

The following morning he asked me to stay after class. All lesson long I sat at my desk and was filled with torturous anxiety. I kept guessing at what he might say to me. Would he like my stories or not? Would he find so many mistakes that I'd feel embarrassed and so stupid I'd give up writing? Would he just treat me like some kid with a silly school project and not take me seriously? I was dizzy from thinking of all the ways he would find it too kidlike.

At the end of class, after the other students had left, I stayed behind and slowly approached his desk. He bent down and pulled my black notebook out of his tote bag.

I was as nervous as if he had pulled out a black bomb.

"Relax," he said warmly as he opened the cover of the journal and flipped to page one of the first story. Then in a teacherly voice he continued, "This is impressive. The stories are good, but they need work. They read like *first drafts*."

"Is that bad?" I asked.

"It's not about good or bad," he replied. "It's about what you have figured out already, and what you haven't. Your structure is good—you have beginnings, middles, and endings. And you have problems, action, and solutions—so you are on the right path."

"But?" I asked.

"You need to work on the *craft* of writing," he said. "On polishing up the sentences and improving the flow of the story one draft at a time. I'll point out some useful tips for rewriting the stories to make them stronger."

"I'd love that," I said. "I want to get better."

"To start with," he said, "let me just say you have plenty of action. Wild action!" He smiled when he said that. "In fact," he continued, "you seem to be a magnet for action—and especially for pain!"

"I think my mother would agree with you," I replied, grinning.

"But there is more to a good story besides action. You

need more dialogue for your characters. And they need to show a little more emotion. And the writing has to have more clarity. And better word choices."

"Okay," I said, and swallowed hard. It seemed like *everything* needed redoing. I opened my language arts notebook to take notes. Once I had a pencil in my hand I said, "I'm ready."

"Rule number one," Mr. Adolino said directly, and looked me right in the eyes. "Don't try to fix everything wrong in the story on the second draft. It's the biggest mistake you can make!"

"Well, how many drafts do I have to do?" I asked, sounding a little wimpy.

He narrowed his eyes and stared into mine as if judging my dedication. "Let's just start with a handful of the essentials," he replied. "But the secret to doing effective drafts is to focus on rewriting *one key layer* of your story at a time."

He could tell by the blank look on my face that I didn't understand what he meant by the word *layer*.

"What I mean," he continued, "is when you do a draft, just pay attention to one element—or one layer—at a time. The first layer might be the *action layer*. Read your story slowly, like a snail, and make sure the reader will see exactly the same action that you see in your mind—as if you were filming your story for a movie. You never want the reader to suddenly get lost in your story and say, 'I don't understand how this character got from point A to point B.' Make everything perfectly clear for the reader."

"Okay, but then what?" I asked.

"When you finish that layer, then go back to the beginning of the story and choose another layer, like the *emotional layer*. This layer shows the reader all the emotions and thoughts inside your characters. You want them to say and do and think things that display their likes and dislikes, and motivations for doing and thinking what they do. For instance, if you have a mysterious stranger move into the house next door to you, your reader needs to know if he is a good neighbor or if he is planning some trouble—and *why*. When you finish getting the insides of all the characters just right, you can focus on another layer."

"How many other layers are there?" I asked. All I could think of was my cousin's wedding cake, which had twenty layers!

"Well, there's the *description layer*. Read your story carefully and make sure all your descriptions are clear. We

want to see what the mysterious stranger looks like—perhaps he is foaming at the mouth and staggering as he walks, and he smells like bad cheese. We want to see his house. If you peek into his window, the reader wants to peek, too. If he has lots of interesting inventions that might change the world for the better, or worse, you have to describe all the details so the reader gets a complete picture of the character and the inside of the house and the inventions."

"A lot of layers," I remarked, panting from taking notes so quickly.

"Just think of it as a wedding cake," he said.

"I already was," I blurted out. "And it was a tall one."

"Remember," Mr. Adolino said, returning to his teacherly voice, "Rome wasn't built in a day. So don't be afraid of a little extra effort. Another layer is dialogue. Making your characters *speak* with pizzazz is important. What if the mysterious stranger is making a movie and when he catches you peeking in the window he says, 'You have the perfect demented face for my zombie movie!' When characters speak in distinctive ways, they *pop alive* in the reader's head and become three-dimensional. In fact, the reader no longer is paying attention to the writer, because your characters have totally captured their attention."

Nothing builds great characters like snappy dialogue that captures the reader's attention and moves the story forward at a fast pace.

As Mr. Adolino spoke, I kept writing like a wild man. I thought my hot pencil point was going to set the paper on fire. Still, this was all good stuff and I didn't want to forget one word of it.

"Finally," he added, "you have the *nuts-and-bolts layer.* This is the layer you pay attention to in order to create a professional-looking draft, one that shows the reader you take pride in your work. You have to slowly read your story and rake out all the words that are junk and clutter and meaningless. For instance, the word *very* should not be used over and over. *Really* is another word that gets overused. And that word *like*! You have to use *like* sometimes, but don't use it in every sentence because you'll end up saying 'This is like that, and that is like this,' and on and on. Remember, if you describe something properly, then it doesn't have to be like anything else. It can simply be *itself.* Sure, you have to work a little harder to find the perfect adjective—but when you do you decorate the story with beautiful words and it becomes a work of art."

"Is that the last draft?" I asked, my voice rising.

He could tell I was overwhelmed. "For now it is," he said.

I sighed with relief.

"Oh!" he abruptly cried out. "One more thing."

"What?" I cried right back.

He smiled. "Don't forget to put your name on your work," he advised. "Practice your signature and make that a thing of beauty, too."

Suddenly he looked up at the classroom clock.

"Ugh," he groaned, and hopped up. "I have a meeting with a grumpy parent. I have to go."

"I bet that will make a good story," I ventured to say.

"I could write a book on this one," he replied, and quickly gathered up his school materials.

"Then maybe you better write it down," I suggested.

He stood there for a minute with an exasperated look on his face. "If I had forty-eight hours in every day," he said, "I could fill my own journal with parent-teacher stories. And it would be a best seller!" He laughed out loud and then he dashed off.

That day I staggered like a zombie out of the classroom with my black book under my arm and my notebook full of advice, and even though I knew I had just made a lot of work for myself, I remembered another thing my mother always said: "Anything worth doing is worth doing well."

My conversation with Mr. Adolino about the layers of writing has stayed with me all these years. Now, as a professional writer, I call my work on these layers *focused drafts*. The layers are pretty much the same as those taught to me by Mr. Adolino, but over time I've made a few basic adjustments.

19

Focused Drafts

He grinned like a dog then
turned up the ~~dail~~ dial. The water
conducted the ~~prickly~~ electricity
to my ~~quivering~~ bottom. ~~I burped.~~
I shot off the chair AND ~~fell~~
~~out the window.~~ I ROLLED head-
over-heels across the FLOOR.
"~~Holy cow~~ "GOOD ONE," I remarked
from the ~~pointy~~ FAR CORNER OF the
Room.
"Jackie!" I heard my mom call...

Often when writing a first draft we write
like we speak. This can be helpful when quickly capturing a story. However, writing as we speak can be a bit
sloppy on the page. As writers, we have to rewrite our
first drafts and then we can refine and polish our ideas
and sentences.

Once you have your first draft in your journal, here is
what you do next: Type up the story on a computer, or
neatly rewrite it by hand. Then start the process of

rewriting your story by working one at a time on the following eight *focused drafts*.

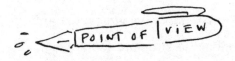

It is important to know who is telling the story. If the story is in the *first person* point of view, then it sounds like this: "I said . . . I did . . . I thought . . ." The voice telling the story is the same voice as the main character. You can also write a story in the *second person* point of view: "You said . . . You did . . . You thought . . ." But the second person becomes tedious and clunky after a while. The *third person* point of view sounds like this: "She said . . . She did . . . She thought . . ." The third person is useful when you have a lot of characters in a story and you want the reader to know what each of them is doing and thinking. When you write about yourself, as I have done in the Jack Henry and Jack Gantos stories, you always use the first person. As Jack Henry would proudly say, "It's all me all the time!"

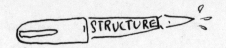

STRUCTURE:

Carefully read your story and make sure you have all the elements of writing in the proper order so that the structure (beginning, middle, end) contains the characters, setting, problem, rising action, climax, resolution (solving the problem), and the double physical and emotional endings.

PHYSICAL ACTION

The physical movement of the characters, animals, and objects in the story must be clear so that readers can "see" what is taking place as if they were watching a film. Action is also tied to each character, so make sure the action is *true* and *believable* for each character. The *rising action* in the middle of the story should be an acceleration of action and excitement to create suspense, get your readers wondering what happens next, and keep them glued to the page.

INTERIOR LIFE

This draft is where you make sure the insides of the characters are fully revealed and understood by the reader. The reader may need to know the motivations, likes, dislikes, and emotions of the characters. This may also include what the characters are thinking and what they are imagining. Remember, the more the writer adds to the character, the better the reader can judge the character's strengths and weaknesses, likes and dislikes. You want your readers to believe in and care about your characters.

DIALOGUE

The dialogue draft is where you allow your characters to speak and represent themselves. Good dialogue builds *fully rounded* characters who come alive and take center stage in the book while the writer recedes into the shadows. Your characters must come alive—and not be shallow hand puppets that belong to you as the writer. Good dialogue captures the reader, reveals character personalities and motivations, and can quickly advance the story action. Dialogue can also be used to create conflict or agreement between characters, or to reveal key information about the story.

DESCRIPTIONS

The descriptions draft is where you take extra care to be both precise and poetic as you describe everything about the setting, the characters' physical life, and their emotional life. Not only do you describe what the characters are looking at, but you also describe how they feel about it. Good description also adds a *mood* to the story. For example, it emphasizes whether something that happens is scary, uplifting, puzzling, boring, mysterious, or nerve-racking.

RIGHT WORDS

With this draft, take a rake and clean out all the extra *very*s and *really*s and *like*s and *just*s and *and*s and *but*s and other little words that sit around your story like all the junk you kick under your bed. Throw that clutter away! Then replace those words with precise vocabulary that adds color and character to your story.

CLEAN UP AND POLISH

Finally, you have to make sure all the spelling is correct and all the punctuation is in place. A good tip is to read your story out loud to yourself. Then you can quickly judge the dialogue and make sure the characters sound true to themselves. Also, when you read your story out loud, you can hear the flow and sense the pace (speed), and you'll notice any halting and stumbling parts. Then you can fix the rough parts and remove any

repetitious parts. Plus, you can add brilliant
new details to dress up your story.

So after I heard Mr. Adolino's sound advice, I bought a
second black book and copied all my stories and rewrote
them so that they had a good structure with all the elements inside. Then I did all my layers, or focused drafts,
as he suggested (and a few more I thought of myself).

My stories were instantly a lot better. Yes, it took extra
effort on my part. But if I got confused, I just asked
Mr. Adolino for advice and he straightened me out. Finally, I rewrote the entire book of stories. When I wrote
my name on the cover I was filled with the kind of pride
that only comes from hard work well done.

Then I went back to the library and, with Mrs.
Hammer's help, put my new-and-improved version of
Jack's Black Book on the shelf. After that, I went to Mr.
Adolino and told him that the book was ready for readers.
He seemed impressed.

This time I only had to wait two days before it
vanished.

I was so excited I told Mr. Adolino.

"Well, has it returned?" he asked.

"Not yet," I replied. "I check every day. Whoever is reading it is taking their time."

"That's probably because it's so good," he remarked.

"You think so?"

"Only time will tell," he replied. "But I have a good feeling that the reader is going to be *impressed*."

Every day I checked the library. And with each passing day, I thought more about the meaning of the word Mr. Adolino had used: *impressed*.

An impression could be either good or bad or so-so. Not only was it a lot of work to write the book, but now I had to suffer even more just waiting to find out what kind of impression it made on the reader.

And then my book showed up in the Book Return box. My heart was pounding as I snatched it from Mrs. Hammer and ran to a quiet corner of the library where no one could see my face. Quickly I flipped it open to the back, where I had once again added a page for "Comments from Readers."

Someone had written a full-page note:

Wow. This book blew me away. There is great action.

DEEP emotions. Captivating
descriptions. Snappy dialogue.
Poetic WORD CHOICES. AND only
a few spelling and grammar
mistakes (but they can be
easily FIXED).

There was only one person at the school who would write those words. At the end of the comment it was signed:

You are under way to being
a great writeR! — MR. Adolino

Yes, I said to myself.

To this day, reading Mr. Adolino's comments has been one of the most satisfying moments of my life, and obviously I have not forgotten the thrill of it.

20

A Parting Surprise

But Mr. Adolino wasn't finished with me yet, and he wasn't finished with the other kids like me— other would-be writers at the school who I didn't know existed. He organized a literary assembly in the school theater and brought together student poets and playwrights, songwriters, comedians, and anyone else who was, like me, secretly scribbling away with hopes and dreams of being a writer.

Before we went onstage at that assembly and read our work, we stood behind the curtain and he gathered us around him. He looked us in the eyes and said in a serious voice, "You writers have to stick together. Start a writing group this summer so you can share work and be supportive. There are times when writing isn't easy, but a good writing friend can help you get through the rough times."

He shook our hands and then he turned to me. "Jack," he said, "you're up first. Take the stage and read your story as if it were the greatest story ever written."

I took a deep breath, stepped out from behind the curtain, and walked to the middle of the stage. The whole school was staring at me. I took another deep breath and looked right back at them.

"My name is Jack Gantos," I said into the standing microphone, "and the title of my story is 'The Watch.'"

And then a feeling came over me, a kind of joyous courage, and I opened my mouth and the words streamed out like golden fish rushing down a river and into the sea.

The Watch

I was in the fifth grade and every morning I took the bus to school. Sometimes I missed the bus and had to quickly run back home from the bus stop and beg my mother for a ride. This always annoyed her, and as she drove me in the car I had to listen to a long lecture about my lack of "personal responsibility."

Well, I had missed the bus again and so I dashed home. My mom was in the kitchen and when I opened the back door of the house she cried out, "Did you miss the bus again?"

"Yes," I said, and pointed up at the kitchen clock. "I think our clock is slow."

"The clock is fine," she replied. "*You* are slow. You just don't know how to manage your time."

"I know, I know," I said apologetically. "But that old clock throws me off. What I need is my own watch." I tapped on my wrist with my finger. "Then I'd know how to pace myself."

She gave me a stern look and put her fists on her hips. "You aren't missing the bus on purpose just so I'll get you a watch," she asked, "are you?"

"No," I replied. "I swear."

"Well, don't get your hopes up for a watch," she said bluntly.

"Betsy has a watch," I ventured to point out.

"That's because your sister is *responsible*," my mother

replied. "To be honest with you, I don't think you are mature enough for a watch."

That really was insulting and I could feel myself getting worked up. "Not *mature* enough?" I shouted. "I'm a very mature boy—especially for my age. Ask anyone."

"I don't have to ask," she said. "I'm your mother. I know everything about you. A watch is a very sophisticated piece of equipment and *you* are *not*."

"Well, you don't know everything," I shot back, "or else you would know what a responsible, mature boy I am. To show you how mature I am, I'll ride my bike to school."

Before she could reply I spun around and stomped to the garage and got my bike out and took off.

"What does she know?" I muttered over and over as I pedaled. "I'm very mature. I'm very sophisticated. Everyone says so." I pedaled like a wild man because my teacher, Mr. Garth, was very strict and didn't like anyone to arrive late and interrupt his lessons. Unfortunately, I was late, but Mr. Garth only gave me a harsh look as I tiptoed to my desk.

After that day, to prove to my mom how mature I was, I kept getting up earlier and eating faster and nervously marching down to the bus stop. I was never sure if I was going to be early or late, but I was certain there was something wrong with the clock, and I suspected my sneaky sister was intentionally setting the time back on the clock in order to make me late and get me in trouble. This made me more and more nervous until one morning I went down to the bus stop so early there were no other kids standing around. Usually there were two or three early birds sharing homework, but now there were none.

"Great!" I said, and kicked at the dirt. "I probably missed the bus again. But if I had a watch I'd know for sure."

Just then, right where I had kicked up the dirt, something shiny caught my eye. I looked down and on the ground there was a watch.

"It's my lucky day," I said, and reached down and picked it up. It was half covered with dried mud, but it was still ticking. I knocked the mud off and read the time and found I was really early.

"Little Watchie"

I put it on my left wrist. It fit perfectly, as if it had always been mine. I pulled out my shirttail and spit on it
and polished the crystal. I watched the thin second hand
spin in a circle. It rotated so smoothly. I was impressed.
And then in a fit of affection I named it "Little Watchie."
And instantly I loved Little Watchie, and as the second
hand circled around I knew he was waving just to me.

"Hello, Jack," he whispered, every minute on the
minute.

"Hello, Watchie," I replied in return, and waved right
back. I could tell we were going to be good friends and
that Little Watchie was going to help me solve my bus-
stop problem.

One by one the other kids showed up at the bus stop,
but I paid no attention to them. I just stared into the
hypnotic round face of Little Watchie, and when I held
him to my ear he whispered, "Tick, tick, tick," like he was
telling me a coded secret.

When the bus arrived at seven-thirty I glanced at Little
Watchie and he was perfectly on time. "Good boy," I said
under my breath, and patted his shiny face. "You are my
new best friend, and you can come with me everywhere
I go." I paid no attention to anyone else on the bus. Little
Watchie was all I needed.

He was a good friend. I was usually late to class because I didn't manage my time correctly and goofed off at my locker, but Watchie was a pro at time management—one glance at him and his friendly face gave me a look that said, "Get a move on." He kept me right on schedule.

In class that day I tried to listen to my history teacher, Mr. Garth, but I was spellbound by Little Watchie. Every few seconds I checked the time. It was so fascinating to measure the world in terms of time. It took only five seconds to take a deep breath and exhale. That meant I breathed twelve times per minute. And that meant seven hundred and twenty breaths per hour, and that meant in an entire day I breathed seventeen thousand, two hundred and eighty times. I slumped down into my chair. *No wonder I'm exhausted all the time,* I thought. *I'm worn out from all that breathing.*

Mr. Garth must have noticed my mind was wandering.

"Jack!" he sharply called out as he aimed the black rubber tip of his pointer stick at me.

That stick scared me. He waved it around like he was an Olympic fencer. He had named it "Mr. Stick." If you crossed your legs while sitting and your foot stuck out into the aisle, he'd strike it with the stick and growl,

"Mr. Stick doesn't like to trip over feet!" If you slumped down into your chair, he'd sneak up on you and spear you in the back. "Mr. Stick doesn't like bad posture," he'd bark as you straightened up. And if you were staring into outer space, he might reach out and, with the flick of his wrist, Mr. Stick would zing your earlobe, which really smarted. "Mr. Stick likes to be listened to," he'd remind you.

He was a menace with that stick, so after he called my name I sat up-right, pulled my feet in tightly under my desk, and jutted my head forward to let him know I was listening.

"Ye-es," I replied, with my voice breaking.

"Yes, what?" he snapped as Mr. Stick stood at attention in his hand.

"Yes, *sir*!" I answered back. By then my breathing was out of control. My heart was pounding and I kept thinking that I was breathing at sixty times per minute. I wanted to glance at Little Watchie and time myself, but I didn't dare look away from Mr. Garth

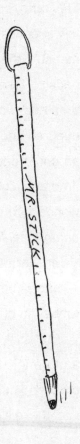

because now that I had caught his attention he began to ask me questions.

"Why isn't your notebook on your desk?" he asked.

"Sorry," I replied.

"Sorry, what?"

"Sorry, *sir*," I said, trying my best to sound respectful and not just terrified. I lifted my desktop and searched for my notebook, which I instantly realized I had left at home, because we were supposed to have memorized "Paul Revere's Ride" by Henry Wadsworth Longfellow. And then I knew what was coming next, which made my breathing speed up even more. I really wanted to look at Little Watchie, but Mr. Garth did not take his piercing eyes off of me.

"Could you please recite the first stanza of Mr. Long-fellow's great historic poem?" he demanded.

His voice was more of a dare than a question. I was sure he believed I couldn't recite it. He always looked at me as if I were never prepared.

I looked up into the air as if the poem had been written on the ceiling and I could read it off with ease. But nothing came to my mind.

"The seconds are ticking off," he reminded me.

I just couldn't help myself. I stretched my arm out and took a quick glance at Little Watchie. The seconds *were* ticking off—for both of us.

Mr. Garth tapped his pointer stick against the palm of his open hand. "I'll give you a hint," he offered. "The first line begins with, 'Listen, my children, and you shall hear.' Now, what is the rest of the stanza?"

I was in trouble. It was as if I'd never heard that opening line before. Never. Then I realized I had memorized the wrong poem. "I'm sorry, sir," I replied as respectfully as possible because Mr. Stick was twitching by his side. "I memorized ''Twas the Night before Christmas.'"

He frowned. "How many times do I have to ask you to write down your assignments?"

There was not a safe answer to that, so I lowered my head. "Sorry, sir," I squeaked.

"Now, take the empty desk at the front of the class," he said, and pointed Mr. Stick at a desk that was next to his and only used for students who had messed up.

It was a place where he could keep an eye on us. But I hadn't really messed up—I just did the wrong homework.

"Pay attention," he commanded, "and you'll learn some history."

I stood up and took a sheet of paper and a pencil with me to the desk. I sat down and got ready to write whatever lines I could that the other students had memorized. But suddenly I remembered Little Watchie, and he was far more interesting than what Paul Revere was telling the man to hang in the belfry of the Old North Church.

To the side of the desk where I was sitting was a tall window with a view of the playing fields. I had my wrist on the desk so that I could keep an eye on Little Watchie. Just then the sun came out from behind a cloud and shone through the window and hit the crystal on the watch, then bounced up and made a small circle of light on the ceiling.

"You are so clever," I said to Little Watchie. He didn't need a candle to send Paul Revere a signal. Little Watchie made his own signal light. He was special. Very, very special.

That is so cool, I said to myself, and right away I forgot all about Paul Revere's exhausting ride to save us from the British. Instead, I looked up at my circle of light and started drawing with it. I played like I was Harold from *Harold and the Purple Crayon* drawing an imaginary city with his little purple crayon. After I finished drawing my city full of clocks and watches, I then wrote my name about a hundred times. Then I just started to zigzag the circle of light back and forth across the ceiling until I ran out of ideas.

Then I thought, *I wonder if I shine this light in some kid's eyes if it will bug him?* Well, there was nothing left to do but try it out. I saw a kid in the front row and he was looking at Mr. Garth with his chin resting on the palm of his hand. I aimed, and fired. The circle of light hit him in the eyes and he started to blink. *Wow,* I thought. *This is so wicked.* I waited for Watchie to tick off ten seconds, and as soon as the kid settled down I did it to him again. Once again he flinched and started to blink and then rub his eyes. He sort of looked puzzled, and annoyed, too.

Watchie is powerful, I said slyly to myself. *Very, very powerful.*

Because I was sitting in front of the class everyone was facing me. I went down the row of kids. *Zap! Zap! Zap!* Before long, I had the first row flinching left and right and rubbing their eyes and squinting as they looked around the room like Paul Revere trying to figure out if he saw one light or two or twenty-two.

Then I worked quickly. I got every-one in the second row. Watchie was a good shot. Finally, I worked my way down the third row, then the fourth. Little Watchie and I had teamed up and gotten them all. Now there was no one left but the teacher.

I took a deep breath and let it out slowly because I knew I was going to have to be very careful.

I waited patiently for Mr. Garth to get into the perfect position for me to zap him with Little Watchie. The trouble was that he kept dashing around the room while trying to terrify everyone into remembering "Paul Revere's Ride." I could never get a really good shot at his eyes. But finally I was in luck. Lynda Swift, who had a totally photographic memory, couldn't stand listening to how everyone else was butchering the poem. She raised her hand, and I guess Mr. Garth couldn't stand listening to everyone else, either, because he knew that once he called on Lynda, Paul Revere's ride would soon be over.

"Yes, Lynda," he said. "Could you please recite the poem the rest of the class has either menaced or forgotten?"

"Yes, Mr. Garth," she replied, and stood up for dramatic effect.

As she clasped her hands and opened her mouth I carefully observed Mr. Garth. He lifted his chin in the air, smiled a big smile, and squinted with pure pleasure.

But not for long. His squint gave me just enough of a sliver of an eyeball to aim for. I twisted my wrist and— *zap!*—got him right in the corner of the eye. Quickly I cupped my free hand over the crystal of Watchie as Mr. Garth's head jerked toward the front of the class. But by then I was entirely focused on Lynda Swift. I was even mouthing the words as they rolled off her tongue. Very sneakily I dared to glance at Mr. Garth. He had Mr. Stick in one hand and was slowly tapping it against the palm of his other as his eyes scanned the room like a prison searchlight.

Lynda Swift knew that she had lost his full attention, and so she stopped reciting. "Do you want me to continue?" she asked.

Mr. Garth turned his eyes toward her. "Of course," he shot back. "Certainly. You are doing a splendid job. Students, pay attention to Lynda."

The students all turned to stare at her, but I was glancing sideways at Mr. Garth. As soon as Lynda started up again he allowed himself to relax and enjoy the poem. That's when I struck.

Zap! I got him right in the same eye!

This time he jerked his head back and in frustration stamped his shoe on the tile floor. Mr. Stick slashed at the air above his head as he glowered at each and every one of us. But I was perfectly poised, with my hand patting the polished crystal on Little Watchie.

I felt so smart. I was so clever. *But don't get carried away,* I said to myself. *Just take it easy.*

Mr. Garth was pretty smart, too. After all, he *was* the teacher. But he made another mistake. By chance, he turned slightly away from me and opened his eyes as wide as they would go. It was the perfect opportunity for me to zap him another good one. But just when I aimed Watchie and blasted the sharp beam of light, Mr. Garth suddenly swiveled his head around and I zapped him right in the middle of his forehead.

He saw the flash of light come off the crystal of Little Watchie and slowly he smiled at me. He had set me up. Then his smile turned into an evil grin and he raised Mr. Stick high above his head.

"Mr. Gantos!" he snapped, and marched directly toward me until he towered in front of my desk. "Let me see that watch!"

I held out my wrist. Little Watchie's sweet round face looked so vulnerable.

"Take off the watch," he instructed, "and put it flat on the desk."

Nervously, I did what I was told.

"Now sit back in your seat," he commanded, and raised himself up onto his toes as his arm and Mr. Stick hovered menacingly overhead.

I sat way, way back. Then, in less than a second, Mr. Stick was slashing through the air. *Bam!* It cracked down on Little Watchie's face and he exploded into a thousand little tiny watch pieces that rained down onto my desk and the floor.

"You'll never do that again," Mr. Garth growled, "now, will you, son?"

"No," I said, staring at the scattered remains of Little Watchie.

"No, what?"

"No, sir," I swiftly replied.

For the rest of the class I sat at the front of the room with my eyes lowered as everyone glared at me. 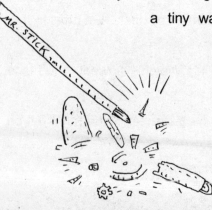 Every now and again I dared to pick up a tiny watch piece—a gear, a spring, a jagged bit of the crystal—and I thought to myself that if I was ever lucky enough to find a watch again I'd definitely *not* be doing *zap, zap, zap* anymore.

It was a long school day for me. When the bell rang I ran to my bus. After it dropped me off at my stop, I slowly followed the sidewalk to my street and eventually up my front walk. I opened the screen door and walked across the living room to the kitchen.

There was my mother—one hand gripping the top edge of a mixing bowl like she was holding it by the ear, and the other hand holding a long wooden spoon in the air.

I looked up at the clock. I still wasn't sure what time it was, but I was totally sure my mother was right—I *wasn't* mature enough for a watch. How pathetic was that?

The End

When I finished reading the students cheered. I took a bow and walked off the stage as a poet stepped out from behind the curtain. I'm sure the poet was great, but I don't remember her poem. I was overwhelmed with the applause and support the students gave me, and I can remember it to this day.

On that special day, all of us young writers thrived

and beamed from the cheers and applause we received. All our effort had paid off. No one thought about how hard it was to get started writing, or to keep up our good writing habits, or to do all the rewriting. That was behind us.

After our school performance some of us did form a writing club, as Mr. Adolino had advised. We met each week and once again worked steadily on our new stories and poems and plays and jokes and songs. We shared our new writing, and we trusted each other and depended on each other's support and friendship.

You may or may not have a writing club, but now you always have me on your side, and this book for guidance

and inspiration. So get a journal, make your lists of possible action ideas and possible emotional ideas, and draw your house map. Put on it where everything interesting happens—big and small, action and emotion—and then set up your daily writing habits. Even a little bit every day will add up. Get the structure (beginning, middle, end) set up with all the elements (character, setting, problem, rising action, crisis, solve the problem, and the all-important double ending: the physical and emotional ending). Afterward, do your focused drafts and polish up your story so that it is a beautiful piece of literary art—and don't forget to sign your name to it.

A Final Word

"I wrote that Book. My name is on the cover. It's mine!"

Thank you for reading this book and for believing in me just as much as I believe in you. There is always a handshake between the writer and the reader that says "I trust you," and this book is my trusting handshake with you. Know that I have faith in you to get the job done, just as you should have faith in yourself. Be smart. Take it one step at a time. Put yourself first in your writing life and write passionately about the stories and characters you care about—that's the *good stuff* that ends up in a book with your name on it.

Finally, I hope that someday I am lucky enough to walk into a library and check out your book, and read it, and be changed by the power and beauty of the language, and the depth of the characters, and the compelling story that holds me in its grip.

I bet it will be *brilliant*!

Writing Connections

Here are three exercises to help you turn on your Writing Radar and build confidence as a storyteller.

Writing Exercise 1

Use your Writing Radar to break down the story "The Watch" (pages 174–189) to its structure and elements, and then check your answers with mine on page 198. You will see what an expert you have become.

Characters

Setting

Problem

Rising Action

<u>Crisis</u>

<u>Resolution/Solving the Problem</u>

<u>Double Ending (always look for a double ending!)</u>
- Physical ending:

- Emotional ending:

Answers to questions on pages 196–197

Characters
My mom, me, Little Watchie, Mr. Garth, Lynda Swift.

Setting
Begins at my house and then shifts to the bus stop, school, and then back to my house.

Problem
I need a watch so I can tell what time it is and not miss the bus.

Rising Action
Starts with me wanting then finding a watch and naming it Little Watchie. I play with the watch. I zap all the kids in class. I zap the teacher twice, and suspense builds up to the crisis.

Crisis
The third time I try to zap the teacher, he catches me.

Resolution/Solving the Problem
My teacher and Mr. Stick solved that problem. *Ka-boom!* Nothing but watch pieces.

Double Ending
- Physical ending: I'm left with nothing but watch pieces.
- Emotional ending: I realize I'm just as immature as my mother thinks I am.

Writing Exercise 2

Draw your hands, both palm side and knuckle side, and write the story of the scars you see there. Splinters. Burns. Double joints. Fingers slammed in car doors. Blood blisters. (Did your mother ever pop a blood blister by sticking a straight pin through the bubble of skin and releasing the skinny stream of blood?)

For some reason, hands are maps of some of the most painful things that have happened to us, or some of the most extraordinary, or evidence of what we do for a living. On my right-hand middle finger I have a deep indentation on the side of the top digit from holding a pen very tightly between that finger and my pointer finger.

Next, draw all your body scars.

I have a faint scar on my chin. Every day when I shave I look at that scar and remember how I got it. One night we were playing flashlight tag in the neighborhood and I was running at full speed between two houses when I ran my face straight into the blunt end of a low tree branch. That really hurt, but it wasn't until I was caught and the flashlight was shone into my face that we all realized my chin was bleeding like an open spigot. My dad was one of those guys who don't believe in getting stitches for a cut. "Just put a Band-Aid on it," he'd say. I did put a Band-Aid on it and so ended up with a great scar.

An even better scar was when I fell down the slippery slope of a seawall on the Intracoastal Waterway in Fort Lauderdale. I was fishing and lost my footing on some sea moss and slid down the wall and into the water. I pulled myself out, but as I walked away I noticed I had sliced my knee open on a cluster of barnacles. Blood was cascading down my shin and filling my sneaker. When my dad saw it he said, "That's a three-Band-Aid cut." Now I have a scar on my knee that looks like a flattened purple worm.

Okay, one more scar. I had just learned how to drive. Or, rather, I should say that I had passed my driver's test though I still had not mastered the art of driving. Anyway, I pulled up to a stop sign and stopped. The road passing in front of me was on a sharp curve, so it was a little tricky to see if a car was coming. I pulled out slowly onto the road and looked to my left. Then I pulled out more and looked to my right. By then someone came around the curve on my left side and plowed right into my door. My car spun in a circle and I was shoved into a palm tree. I hit my head on something solid and got a good long gash on my skull. I had to crawl out my driver-side window. When the other driver approached me and saw my bloodied head—which by then looked like a bloody neck stump—he passed out. I staggered over to him like a zombie and dropped to one knee to help out and when he opened his eyes and saw me he screamed bloody murder. As he jumped up I fell off to one side. He ran hollering to a nearby house. Anyway, I was taken to a hospital, where my hair was shaved and I was given stitches. Had he been there, my dad would have called the gash a "dozen-Band-Aid cut." My hair grew back and still hides the scar, but if I ever go bald I'm going to look like someone hit me with a meat cleaver.

Remember, your body is like a page in a notebook filled with random drawings—scars, missing teeth, braces, bad tattoos, no hair, funky feet, really weird belly buttons, crutches, wheelchairs, and more. Just think if you are the person with two different eye colors. All of these individual features and conditions are part of your individuality—and what is singular about you is always worth writing about.

Writing Exercise 3

Draw two circles that will each be the face of a clock. Fill in the numbers, one through twelve. One clock face will be the morning hours, and one will be the evening hours. Then, every hour on the hour that you are awake, write down your strongest emotions.

Often a story begins with an *action*, an *event* that can been seen. For example, someone throwing up their colorful lunch in a classroom would be an action. Walking into your house on your birthday and having all your friends yell "Surprise!" would be an action. A mean pit bull chasing you down the street is an *action*.

But just as often (and sometimes overlooked), good stories begin with a strong emotional feeling. So on your clock face you might have written *disgusted* at 1:00 p.m. because someone threw up in class. Then at 6:00 p.m. you might have written *thrilled* because after your extra-long piano lesson on your birthday you walk into your house and there is a surprise party for you. Or at 8:00 a.m. you write *fearful* because a careless neighbor's pit bull decides it wants to eat you for breakfast and chases you down the street.

As a writer you are always looking for inspiration. Quite often you find it hiding behind a powerful emotion. And all you have to do is ask, "Why did I feel *grumpy* at 10:00 a.m. today?" or "Why did I feel like a *genius* in math class?" The answer to a question will often lead you to the beginning of a great story.

The Jack Henry Adventures

The five Jack Henry books contain dozens of off-the-wall stories taken straight from the pages of Jack Gantos's own childhood journals. From killer alligators and a duck with backward feet to secret crushes and a hot-pepper-eating contest, these stories are filled with all kinds of funny characters and oddball events that you have to read about to believe.

**"These are the unsaid things that
go on inside kids' brains."**
—Rosie Peele, age eleven

"I suggest you read these books."
—Tristan Sanders, age fourteen